...ng Arts International
...ol. 1, Part 2, pp. i–ii
...s available directly from the publisher
...opying permitted by license only

Mart
Tel:

ontents

Note: With the exception of papers from Maggie Semple, Joan-Ann Maynard, Michael McMillan and Stuart Taylor and the review by Patrick Campbell, the presentations and articles published in this edition are edited transcriptions of audio-recordings.

A. R. T.

Performing Arts International
1996, Vol. 1, Part 2, pp. 1–7
Reprints available directly from the publisher
Photocopying permitted by license only

Re-imagining History: An Introduction to the Black Theatre Conference Papers

A. Ruth Tompsett

Principal lecturer in Drama, Middlesex University.

This special issue of Performing Arts International makes more widely available the papers and presentations from the Black Theatre in Higher Education Conference, held in London in April 1994 (organised by Hazel Carey and myself). It offers the reader a chance to engage in debates on topical issues, to widen their knowledge and understanding of black performance and to catch something of its spirit from the combination here of critical comment, practitioner insight and personal testimony.

The question that arose at the conference was not so much, 'why a Black Theatre Conference?' as 'Why hasn't there been a conference like this one before?' Everyone felt the need for putting black theatre and performance on the educational map. The immediate stimulus for the conference came from experience of Black Theatre Studies at Middlesex University where Hazel Carey and I have been teaching two Black Theatre modules since 1989: the first focuses on African-American and African Theatres, the second on Black and Asian British Theatre. Although aligned to the B.A. performing arts, and thereby attracting dance, music and drama students, cross-accreditation allows students of English Literature, Media and Cultural Studies and Studies in Race and Culture to choose these modules, which makes for especially rich and lively discussion and exchange of insights. There are usually about equal numbers of black and white students, though generally more women than men (an imbalance that tends to be usual in performing arts courses). The content includes study of text together with examination of themes and issues and consideration of aesthetics and form. The module is taught substantially through practical and/or interactional activity and with recognition for the fundamentally integrated nature of black arts; students are encouraged to draw on music, movement and dance in exploring play text and performance poetry and for the final assessment can devise their own interdisciplinary work, drawing from dance, music and drama, and the media and visual arts. The unusual range of studies that students come from enlarges and enriches the scope and quality of the study undertaken and the creative work achieved.

Central to the teaching of both modules is the teaching of texts and themes within a socio-historical context. It can be assumed, in teaching theatre and performance generally, that the cultural and historical contexts to what is studied are familiar to students; whether through history and literature studies at school, through personal reading or from television, film and newspapers and their supplements, the reference points for the greater part of performing arts study belong to a framework that is so familiar it is taken for granted. Exactly the reverse is the case in black theatre studies; for most of us educated in Britain, black and white, the given cultural and historical knowledge and perspectives which frame our interpretation of life and art are narrowly eurocentric; in education and the media, the validity and authenticity of other perspectives are rarely acknowledged. Access to the motivation and meaning of much black performance, whether dance, drama or music, is increased and enhanced where there is knowledge and understanding of a wider historical and cultural context. The study of black theatre needs to be undertaken with openness to different reference points and contexts. Errol John's *Moon on a Rainbow Shawl* and Trish Cooke's *Running Dream*, for example, present human aspirations and dilemmas which have universal resonance, but which also connect to a context of colonial history that is informed from a black perspective.

Students who take these modules tend to engage very fully with the module content. Since most of the material does not appear elsewhere on syllabi it is fresh to students, and because it often raises issues, there is much debate in class and students ask genuine questions of each other and recognise each other as resources of learning. Much of the learning is in common, but sometimes racial diversity within the class makes for distinct kinds of learning. Black students speak of finding it confidence-building to work with material with which they can more immediately identify and from which they can gain a sense of themselves. White students want to know about texts, issues and genres they are conscious of being ignorant about. The art of becoming, of taking parts within black texts for example, can be a revelation to white students, just as black students may feel empowered by such activity. The arts deal with truths and personal realities, and in black theatre studies material can be revealing, even uncomfortable for some; analysis of art works and debate that arises can be strongly pursued and at times painful; the very exclusivity of the higher education syllabus in the arts, which is rarely open to, or aware of, the culturally diverse perspectives and experience of its constituency, mean that where space is made for those diverse perspectives it is difficult for some to feel the relevance or truth of them.

It can be disorienting to have your sense of a fixed reality challenged. Of course for many others, the same experience is generative and energising.

The predominant response from students is one of enjoyment and growth; both in class and in the anonymous feedback questionnaires, students speak frankly about their difficulties in having their view of the world challenged and with excitement about their learning and sense of personal development. The feedback points to the value and validity of studying black performance and writing and of addressing culturally diverse forms and aesthetics. Whether such study needs to be undertaken separately is open to question and debate. Much art work of value and importance is being ignored that belongs within the mainstream syllabus. The dramatic writing of Lorraine Hansbury and August Wilson, for example, needs to be given its place in any module on Naturalism; study of contemporary live art in Britain is partial without inclusion of such black artists as Susan Lewis, Stuart Taylor or Keith Khan. Black theatre is where contemporary political theatre is happening. For people interested in just such broadening and opening up of the syllabus, the conference aimed to be an introduction.

So it was from the experience of teaching black theatre and from student responses to it, that the motivation came for organising the conference, and also its rationale. From her freelance teaching Hazel Carey was aware how rarely black arts are studied in performance training or higher education, and how often students feel short-changed by that. We had heard black practitioners speak of how alienated they had sometimes felt at the exclusively white or eurocentric perspectives they had experienced in their own education or training; they expressed interest in having a teaching role themselves and sharing with others their experience and knowledge. This, then, was our conference constituency. We aimed to bring together teachers, practitioners and students, within the performing arts, to share experience, interests and concerns, and to learn from each other about the developoment of black theatre in Britain and its place in, and potential for, educational study. To make fullest use of our own experience and to avoid the over-generalisation that can arise from spreading too wide, we put the focus on tertiary education, while welcoming interested secondary teachers.

We were also guided in our planning for the conference by the nature of black theatre itself, particularly in recognising its integration of forms and its greater interaction between 'audience' and 'performer' than is usual in traditional western theatre. Theatres of African/Asian derivation or influence tend to draw freely and holistically from performance skills and languages which are not seen as belonging only and separately to dance, drama, music or visual arts. For example within the same piece of theatre, meaning is made as instinctively and readily from movement as from spoken text.

This confounds critics and academics alike, whose own trainings, education and working briefs, apart from less tangible considerations like personal aptitudes, loyalties and ways of seeing, incline them to invest in recognising the arts as existing in separate disciplines and whose receptiveness to integrated work may be restricted. In teaching black theatre, I find myself often referring, rather, to black performance, to embrace its holistic nature, or, to use a westen-perspective term, its interdisciplinarity.

It was important to the conference organisers that criteria for selection of speakers fully took account of the distinctive nature of black theatre in this respect. The majority of speakers were drawn from practitioners who work integratedly across art forms and have training in more than one discipline. For example, the work of Tara Arts draws from dance, music, visual arts and drama and its performers are multiply trained across these disciplines; Maggie Semple, Head of Education at the Arts Council of England, is an arts educator who is a trained and experienced dancer and choreographer; Stuart Taylor's present work is in digital and media art – his training in visual arts and dance; Michael McMillan, who started out as a playwright, now works very much in live art, a performance genre which attracts black creative artists across the board on account of its interdisciplinarity; these are just four examples from the conference contributors.

Anyone attending black theatre performances with black or well-mixed audiences will be familiar with that otherwise rather rare phenomenon in present-day British theatre, the interactional audience. Black audiences and black performance tend to retain a greater sense of theatre's origins in community acitivity and ritual; listening and watching is combined with comments of approbation or disapprobation, with responses indicating recognition of common experience, offering encouragement to or intervention on, the action. Black audience members are participants in black theatre performance. It felt appropriate that the conference should operate in a similarly interactional manner and spirit. Amongst audience/participants were experienced and wise practitioners, and amongst speakers were recent young graduates, at the start of their careers; the conference established from the start a sense that information and learning were two-way, and indeed every input incorporated, and was followed by, animated debate amongst speakers and participants, so that such discussion became as much the matter of the conference as the papers and presentations, as key points were picked up and developed – in the sessions, on the stairs, over meals and coffees. John Adam Hall, University of London, proved a friendly and comfortable venue, which facilitated interaction. The plenary sessions took place in the common room where we were able to organise seating around, and close to, speakers, so that contact and exchange were easy and the podium/auditorium division, with its implied hierarchy, was reduced or even dissolved. Such logistical details, by no means incidental, can be paralleled with the ways in which performance can be staged to break down audience/performance exclusivities, to make theatre an interactional experience and allow for communality.

All the papers and presentations of the conference are offered here. They include inputs on definitions, the aesthetics debate, arts education, arts administration, the black theatre canon, and life stories which trace connections and chart possibilities.

Jatinder Verma, Artistic Director of Tara Arts and the first keynote speaker, was invited to offer a definition or definitions of black theatre and to address the question of a black aesthetic. His contribution offers a robust response; he makes a rigorous and well-argued case for black theatre as distinctive, with its own aesthetic, and states the essential necessity of 'approaching black theatre as an aesthetic phenomenon,... not as a social phenomenon'.

The second keynote speaker, Philip Hedley, Artistic director of Theatre Royal, Stratford East, opens with a very personal statement about where he is coming from. As an audience member commented in ensuing discussion: 'It's not often that someone who addresses you at a Black Theatre Conference admits to being a white racist!' Through a lively combination of anecdote and specific reference, Philip Hedley points to key ways in which a venue and its artistic director and staff can significantly support black theatre development by having in place, and operating, positive attitudes and policies. He especially illustrates the importance of making the performance space available, without interference, to individuals and companies who are not provided for elsewhere, and of looking for new and more relevant ways to promote black performance. His practice is rooted in the sense of a 'continuous loop' between a theatre and its community.

In the third keynote address, 'Arts Education and Cultural Diversity', Maggie Semple, Director of Education and Training at the Arts Council of England, identifies issues, principles and debates that are central to consideration of the role of education in addressing, and indeed embracing, the cultural diversity of Britain. Her wide-ranging deliberations are clearly informed by her past experience as a teacher, a dancer and a choreographer, as well as from her present work at the Arts Council.

These three papers are intended to address the key subject areas of art theory, theatre production and arts education, respectively, as they relate to black theatre. The four shorter inputs from the first Panel, are specifically planned to provide information and insights on present practice, from those who are 'at the rock face'. Sita Brahmachari, Education Officer with Talawa Theatre Company, draws on her immediate experience, and highly successful practice, of bringing young people and live theatre together. Adjoa Andoh, through personal anecdote and reference to professional experience, provides us with insight on some particular attitudes and demands a black actress may encounter from directors, producers and other arts personnel in the (white) establishment and offers a resonant example of standing firm and getting heard. As an experienced director, Joan-Ann Maynard is in a strong position to review black writing for theatre. She presents, here, a valuable selection of play texts many of which are available in published form for study or production, grouping them by theme and thereby indicating something of black theatre's range of concerns and subject-matter, as well as suggesting its distinctive nature. Finally, on this panel, through tracing significant developments in his own artistic life, Michael McMillan ranges over important developments in black British theatre history, identifying influential practitioners, both contemporary and from the past, here and from the Americas; in outlining the shift in his personal artistic development from playwright to live arts practitioner, he points to larger trends in theatre development and to distinctive features of black performance.

The presentations from the Young Practitioners Panel bring us to the heart of the conference's focus, the interface between the education system and the culturally diverse reality of British arts, and do so in the most telling and informing way by giving us a chance to hear from those who have recently graduated, and who are therefore most intensely aware of how arts education does, or does not, address Britain's richly diverse cultural heritage. Each of these four speakers, within a short period of graduating, has already demonstrated remarkable achievement and success in the career they have chosen; their talks take the form of personal testimonies, which conference delegates found both revealing and inspiring.

Common themes emerge as one reads from paper to paper. For example, speakers variously contribute to a definition of a distinctive aesthetic in black arts; the importance of finding different ways of promoting black arts and reaching new, unprovided for audiences also surfaces as a widely recognised concern; thirdly, the social function of black theatre is repeatedly illustrated and substantiated, an aspect that points up black theatre's critical connection to a wider historical context. During the Conference itself, the theme most often returned to in discussion was one that Hazel Carey had presented in her brief opening address:

Black Theatre is a place where we can re-examine and re-imagine history. It feels like a place where each person can feel proud in this multi-racial, culturally diverse land of ours.

The notion of black theatre as a place for 're-imagining history', caught fire with people, who clearly found in it a motivation for themselves and a rationale for their own creativity and learning.

This description or definition of black theatre became an unconsciously agreed agenda for those present at the conference. Just as recognition of the historical context is identified above as critical in black theatre study, so, in the papers that follow, the strong element of personal testimony, is important to both the communication and understanding of the critical debates on black theatre presented in the conference. Adjoa Andoh's reference to some of her personal experiences as an actor point up the 'mis-imagining' of white history; she vividly illustrates how often the characters a black actor is given to play require those actors to mis-shape themselves to fit the white historical perspective that informs much British writing.

A person's sense of self and their understanding of their identity is intimately connected with knowledge of the larger history they are a part of. Where the dominant and established record of how things were, and of how things are, has invisibilised or 'mis-imagined' so much, the arts have a powerful and complementary role in re-imagining history. There is an urgency in black theatre connected to a strong sense of purpose. Black art work, in terms of forms and aesthetics, challenges existing norms and ways of seeing; it enhances and enriches contemporary arts development. For students and teachers, and for critics and practitioners alike, to study, attend or participate in black theatre is to be engaged in a contemporary arts reality which is inherently culturally diverse and wonderfully the richer for being so.

Performing Arts International
1996, Vol. 1, Part 2, pp. 9–21
Reprints available directly from the publisher
Photocopying permitted by license only

Towards a Black Aesthetic

Jatinder Verma

Artistic Director, Tara Arts Theatre Company.

Jatinder Verma was the founder nearly two decades ago of the enterprising and innovative Tara Arts, the leading Asian British Theatre Company. He is an acclaimed theatre director of rich experience. His work ranges from community theatre to large scale productions at the Royal National Theatre. He is also a leading thinker on contemporary theatre development in Britain. In her introduction, Hazel Carey spoke of Jatinder Verma as 'a modern Ulysses' African-born, living in Britain, working in India, Australia, Japan, hopping from continent to continent. 'He draws talent from the people he journeys with, while offering wisdom through his contact with reality'.

I noticed when I came here that in the conference programme, it suggests that I'm going to be talking about words: the definition of a black aesthetic. That was frightening the daylights out of me. Yes I will move towards that with something which is a tentative suggestion, but I'd like to start by posing the question which I posed to myself over the last few weeks: Why should there be Black Theatre Studies in Higher Education, indeed why should we bother with black theatre at all?

It seemed to me, as I posed myself that question, that it was important to get a sense of why we are bothering with it, and when I say 'we' I don't necessarily mean those of us who are practitioners of black theatre, but those of us in some sense or other who are consumers, be it funding bodies, institutions like Middlesex University, venues or indeed the general public. It seemed to me that there are several reasons for supporting black theatre, amongst which is the underlying rationale that it is a good thing, like giving pennies to the homeless, or to other charities, out of a sense of obligation. I don't in any way want to descry that. Another reason, which is not too far from this sense of social obligation, is that the country's education and the arts, ought to reflect the cultural plurality of Britain. This forms a vague part of an equally vague concept-multi-culturalism; there is a kind of social imperative that we're all engaged in trying to promote multi-culturalism. I want to argue that the social imperative for the study, practice, and consumption of black theatre, is wrong, if only because it paradoxically undermines not only the nature of black theatre, but by extension, the reality of multi-culturalism itself; quite simply it detracts from a consideration of black theatre as an *aesthetic* phenomenon and therefore denies it its proper place in the pantheon of British Theatre movements.

Now I want to illustrate this argument by citing recent discussions in The Guardian, for being a do-gooder myself I too read that kind of classic liberal paper. A couple of weeks ago there was a very good article by Richard Gott, where he argued that English culture is now a pale reflection of American culture. It's a point that has been picked up by, amongst others, Anthony Everett ex-secretary general of the Arts Council and Michael Billington who in a recent article posed the question 'What is the job of the National Theatre?' Billington begins unequivocally 'To present the best of world drama'. In the ensuing article, however, his definition of world drama becomes clearer: German, Spanish, Russian plays. The World, as seen through the eyes of one of our leading theatre commentators, is bound by W.A.S.P. America to the west and the Urals to the east. Asia and Africa do not exist. Derek Walcott and Rabindranath Tagore, despite both winning the Nobel Prize for literature, do not exist in the world of drama, nor of course do Wole Soyinka, Girish Karnad, Kali Dasha, Chikamatsu, to name only a few living and classic writers of Asian and African Drama.

Now I keep on asking myself: why this lack? It's too easy to say well they're racist and so forth; I don't think that's good enough as an answer. It seems to me that the lack is because this area of theatre, which all the commentators know about, is still tinged with the air of social phenomenon. Yes, for reasons of equity we ought to have more black work in other words, we ought to promote a greater sense of the real society in Britain today, and in so doing, one forgets that in fact that is part of a cultural phenomenon which is very important. The thing that struck me about Richard Gott's article was that, while on the one hand the thesis is quite acceptable and I have no great problems with it, that yes to a large extent, English culture today is being dominated by America and there is a sense of us being a pale imitation of America, it singularly fails to consider what is going on today in England, the plurality here, and, for example, to consider that the greatest redefinition of the English language that is occuring today is occurring through writers like Salman Rushdie and Ben Okri.

Such writers are reconstituting English. It is the best form of English today without question. And it is not because they sell a lot. Read it, it is the best, it is the most vital English happening today. Look at popular music, what is happening to popular music today? The energy that is coming out of popular music, is, if you like, or certainly I would put it, a black energy, a sense of a free eclectic mix. When I look at, to cite one example, someone like Apache Indian, what I find interesting is that he uses a mode of music coming from African-America. The texture of the language is English and something else,

Punjabi. Why bother with the Punjabi? I mean the kids are only interested in just ordinary music, why bother with this thing? But Apache Indian bothers, he has to bother because the audience wants the odd word that is going to make them feel that this is their essential Englishness, an Englishness which in some ways is also harking to some other space, which therefore gives a wholeness to their lives. Music is being redefined. Text is being redefined.

When I consider dance, I recently watched Shobana Jeyasingh do her choreography to Henry Purcell's music. Now Purcell is not my favourite musician, nor my favourite composer, in fact I've never liked him until I saw this dance. Shobana Jeyasingh's choreography suggested in a way a sense of the Baroque, and for the first time, this music, which has always seemed so superficial to me, so thin, took on depth; here was a dancer coming from on entirely other tradition, one rooted in the earth, who was trying to suggest space just through the movement of an arm, to which a moment in the music gave depth and you began to feel emotion for it. Well that was my response. The point is that here is a redefining going on, here is a vitality of English Culture happening and I stress the point that it is uniquely English. The kind of work that is emerging here could not have happened elsewhere. It is happening because of the peculiar energies that we are facing here; it is an artistic movement, and until we see it as an artistic movement, our commentators, who in some ways are our definers, be we students or be we practitioners, will ignore it, will marginalise it as purely a social necessity and not as an art in itself.

Yet, having made all these points, I am having to face the question: Well alright then, if you're so passionate about the fact that there is an emerging aesthetic, what is the aesthetic of multi-culturalism, or more specifically, what is an aesthetic of black theatre? Well I think the situation we find ourselves in is that we are having to both practice and articulate our theory. What I suggest is not by any means applicable all over the place, but it's what makes sense to me. I have developed a word which to me suggests the framework within which I consider my own work, or at least all black theatre work, and that's the word 'Binglish'.

Having tried that out on several people, they have thought it means Barmy English, or Black English, or Being English. Yes, these are all entirely relevent. I began to think within this term because of what I was seeing in black theatre and what I'm seeing is that even when we are working in English, and most of us are, we find it is impossible to resist our own langages, our own modes of speaking seep through. In our case it's a bit of Punjabi which will come out, we cannot resist, we cannot remain confined within the kind of received sense of English speech, we will always push against it, and it became glaringly obvious when I watched our *King Lear* televised. What was going on as far as my ear could judge was different speech patterns. By design or by accident there is a way in which we speak English which is irresistible to us, which manifests itself in our work, which of course creates problems for others, but that's tough! I think that what it does is lay the groundwork of forming our own langauage of the theatre.

I am now talking about the spoken language, the text language, however what is also observable in black theatre is another kind of inability to resist. In black theatre productions, which have by and large adopted the convention of English realism, the productions are unable to stop themselves from balking against that condition, so then a bit of ritual comes in or a bit of music comes in or movement. These are all attempts at saying that this form is too confining. We stretch ourselves against it. Every single theatre I have seen so far within this areas has refused to remain within the confines established by the conventions of English theatre. This suggests again to me that there is a sense of English. There's a sense of wanting to develop one's own form on one's own terms.

Now it's an axiom, which some treat as racism but I think is also the truth, that we black peoples love to sing and we love to dance. Well yes! Quite right we do. Our imaginations are also rooted in song and dance, in other words, in the unqualified sense of the body at play, in the entire body speaking. If there is one truism one can make, or one stereotype of English Theatre, it is that the body is nowhere to be seen. Acting is from the neck up. I'm not necessarily saying that this is the whole truth, but there is that view. We have not been able to be participants in that in any real sense, we always balked against it. I believe now (even if you quibble with my term Binglish) that what is going on through the resistance to the English convention of theatre is that we are laying the groundwork of our own aesthetic.

Therefore where the new work is perceived then the challenge is to develop the critical vocabulary that can see that work. That means throwing down a challenge to everyone else: you must know or be aware of a multiplicity of languages when you come to black theatre. You must have your ear open to the fact that the English you hear is not necessarily the Queen's. Now I believe we can see this corrupted in a National Theatre production called *Wicked Yaar*, which was about young people in the North of England. Textually, English was constantly being negotiated with Punjabi phrases. Now it was produced by a white director. I have no quarrel with that, I don't think only black people can do black plays, but I do think that if you're going to do such a play, a multicultural play, a black play, the onus of obligation is upon you to know what you are doing. The Punjabi I heard, which undoubtedly was just phrases, the odd phrase, was atrocious in the extreme. Of course people will say that that was the actor's fault – it is not the actor's fault. The director's job is to make sure the language is clear. It doesn't matter whether you understand the language or not, there are many examples of directors working in foreign languages who can still get clarity, so it is a fault with even one word wrong. Unfortunately there were a large number of Asians there and whenever the Punjabi was heard you could see them squirming in their seats and mumbling 'how awful'. Now I make the point only to say what's happening here is complex, this is not a straightforward play, though it has all the appearance of a straightforward play about young people and the problems they face in the North of England. It was done in more or less naturalistic convention. As if reviewing it, one would have to say, yes, but there are two languages in operation here and the Punjabi has a certain ambience which must be taken into account. Then, to look at the music: over the past hundred years or so, English Theatre conventions have separated music from dance, and dance has been separated from theatre altogether. Theatre is left as the art or the arena of the actor speaking. When plays combine music and dance speech in multi-layered texts then how do you judge them? We have to develop the critical vocabulary which is able to see that totality because it's in that totality that we exist.

Yogesh Bhatt (left) and Bhajartee Bai in Tara Arts' production of *Heer Ranjha*, adapted and directed by Jatinder Verma, 1992. Photograph by Hugo Glendinning.

Black theatre is also an arena for re-imagining history, for re-inventing history, quite right, of course it is, but what's the point of re-inventing and re-imagining when there aren't the critical terms by which you can view it? Thus, that re-invented history will always be considered 'ah well, it's a bit of a fable'. Like I was told recently when I said 'Well in fact the French ruled a part of India from the latter part of the 17th Century right through to 1945' – Ah! now come on that's a myth' – it bloody ain't! Had Clive not beaten Dupleix in a sea battle India would have been French like the Cameroons so we'd have all spoken French, but here is this enclave which is French and so

Muraly Menon as Asif, servant to Peter Singh Undarzi, in Tara Art's production of Gogol's *Government Inspector*, adapted and directed by Jatinder Verma, 1990. Photograph by Coneyl Jay.

Shelley King as Heer in Tara Art's production of *Heer Ranjha*, adapted and directed by Jatinder Verma, 1992. Photograph by Hugo Glendinning.

Vincent Ebrahim as Hector (left) and Nirmal Chandra Pandey as Ajax in Tara Art's production of *Troilus and Cressida*, adapted and directed by Jatinder Verma, 1993. Photograph by Hugo Glendinning.

a language developed there which was French and Indian, an extraordinary mixture. This is not a figment of my imagination, it's a part of history. Whose history? Much like one would then have to say to Michael Billington and people like that, which world are you talking of? When I look at the atlas I see quite a large part of the world but your idea of the world seems to be really only Northern Europe, and a little bit to the west, you know, past that lake the Atlantic, and then that's the end of the world.

Now if we are going to address these questions, the point I am making is that the only way we can address these questions is approaching black theatre as an *aesthetic* phenomenon, a theatrical phenomenon, not as a social phenomenon. I accept that it was a social, by extension political, impulse which led to the development of the black theatre scene as we know it today. Our own history is absolutely a part of that, there is no denying that, but if it is not going to remain a marginal experience then it must be seen by

Andrew Mallett as Troilus (top) and Yogesh Bhatt as Cressida in Tara Art's production of *Troilus and Cressida*, adapted and directed by Jatinder Verma, 1993. Photograph by Hugo Glendinning.

ourselves, as much as we insist others see it, as an aesthetic art form in itself, making great demands of language, of modes of speech and of form, and that, I would suggest, is the only healthy way forward.

Otherwise, the only contribution we'll have made in times to come will be cited in sociology books. No, this is a theatrical phenomenon. Wole Soyinka was here in the 1960's and did a play at The Court but no-one acknowledges that of course, and that was well before this movement began. We're talking about one of our greatest writers in the English language who just doesn't exist except as a kind of exotica. And we have Chekhov thrown down our throats ad nauseum. I am not denying Chekhov's greatness. But how come Chekhov has become so quintessentially English? After all he's Russian, a Russian peasant. Why is it so difficult for a play by Wole Soyinka to become English? Here I think we have to think of race, because one mind-set says 'Oh well, we have an African or Asian play we'll need African or Asian actors and there aren't many around'. Do you think we need Russian actors to do Chekhov? I mean there is an equivalence in all cultures, in all societies of history. All societies have gone through similar types of developments, you can find peasants everywhere in all times. I would certainly argue that the kind of peasant experience in Africa and Asia is far closer to the Russian peasantry than ever it was in English history.

Really, this has been a kind of plea because I feel it in myself, and I'm questioning my own practice, and until I can see our work as a specific distinctive language then there is no contribution at all. In a sense, it could almost be as if I'm suggesting a return to separatism - I am. I make no bones about that because there is no question of integration, that is very plain. There is no question of it, and I think it's a completely wrong premise, you have to see it as distinctive languages which are distinctively English and it's that that is the reality of multiculturalism in England. We're not all trying to flatten out and be like each other, because then what's the point? Nothing particularly interesting in that. What is interesting, to make an analogy with foods, is that one has a particular kind of diet which has got a particular kind of ingredient which changes things. There is a little story of Mauritius, which is a French and English island. The French brought their great cuisine, including their roasts, but it was the adding of the chilli on top of the French roast that made it true to them and part of their reality. It developed the cuisine a bit, gave it piquancy that it didn't have before, made for greater chats around the table. Now it's just in these metaphoric ways that cultures have been enriched, not by flattening out but by actually maintaining distinction. That is why black theatre is a distinctive *aesthetic* phenomenon.

Jatinder Verma Answers Questions

Q: What makes it Black Theatre?

A: I would suggest it's a text. My sense of theatrical text is not just speech, but the kind of presentation of it. So it is also form. I think that in those two lies the nature of Black Theatre. In some ways it is constantly in negotiation with the mainstream of life.

Q: What are the starting points at the moment?

A: I think starting points really have to depend upon people, I'm certainly suggesting that there is a multiplicity of languages of theatre, spoken language as much as the language of presentation, which in combination makes black theatre. It doesn't really matter whether one is doing Chekhov or Wole Soyinka. But there is a kind of texture I think it unlikely a white actor would be able to bring to it.

I'm not saying it's not possible, but on the face of it I think it's something that is actually emerging from within black practitioners themselves, because they feel it, whether consciously or subconsciously. They're faced with it all the time by their actors and indeed by their own imaginations, they just don't seem to be able to rest in the sort of confines of the English island, or the confines for the purely western definition of what drama is. So I think that my suggestion would be that it is the multiplicity of languages which defines black theatre. Content, could be whatever you want, as is the prerogative of all theatre, you just raid whatever you think is suitable when you want to produce a play.

Q: Your definition of black theatre is up to the individual, because we're talking about coming from, Asia, Africa and so on, China. To put it under one heading offers a bit of a narrow spectrum. I think that you made a very good point with Binglish. You could be stepping onto new ground. I think this is like a foundation process, because over the 90's it's only just evolved and just coming into education. I see that with London being the only city which has really got a multicultural people in it, and other cities around England haven't, that what comes out of London is the next thing to develop in the smaller counties. It's just like a unique cell being in this area of the country, so it's like this is a learning process we're developing now.

A: Can I just make two points on what you've said, one is that I think London is not that unique. A lot of other cities, in fact throughout the country, are as plural as London is. I think that the extent of theatre we see in London cannot be seen in Birmingham or Manchester, to that extent I agree with you, but other than that, I think there are changes in population in the major cities of England, there is no question of that. In that sense, London is not unique.

Second, as far as the point you made about black theatre, I understand what you are saying, however, I think that conceptually, and that was the only reason I used the term black theatre, conceptually it is possible to talk about a term or to use a term which overhangs all the variety of theatres because there's one thing in common, be they practitioners from China, or Korea or Turkey or Africa or the West Indies or India or Pakistan, it doesn't really matter, or be they born here of parents who are from elsewhere, one thing holds them all together: they're all minorities in this country, yes, they're all seen as not quite English. You can use the word 'ethnic', I have no problems with that , I think ethnic has unique connotation. I'd say the Cornish are ethnics in some sense, the Welsh are ethnics in some sense in England, but we use the term quite specifically. I mean it is a term which is very much related to non-European peoples. Now whatever one might say in terms of equivalence of, say, for example the Jewish experience in England, and of other migrants, one factor alone distinguishes that and that's the factor of colour. That is unique, that is something, which England has not really confronted.

In other respects, I think that we do share similarities with the experiences of other migrants to the British Isles, but this is one aspect which distinguishes them and has continued to. Now I remember in the 70's when we started our company, our hope was that this was just something which was our kind of angst. To people being born after us, those growing up here, you know in 20–30 years time , this would all be passe, it would all be fine. That's the greatest sadness. The only difference I have seen between the 70's and the 90's is in the 70's any racial incident was broadcast loud and clear, I mean it was in the papers and on TV. Now it's not . It's not that obvious, reading through the media, but it is in fact happening to an even greater extent. I think this is one of the greatest theatrical topics facing us at the moment: the nature of change in England, and this is for theatre as a whole, not just specifically for us.

What is the relationship that has made us so twitchy with each other, what makes us not actually join hands? For that we have to look into the Empire because that was where it was founded, that relationship between people, and that's also where it was perverted. That is the nature of England. There is another aspect which is very important in England today and that is a kind of sense of nostalgia, and nostalgia is rooted in loss, loss of Empire, loss of a central position in the World. I think in that, white and black are common. The difference only is this: we have accepted the loss, I certainly do. I know I have no home, I know I never will have a home, in the sense that a home is connected to whose language I speak, whose soil I am a part of, where I am born, where I am nourished, whose culture I am a total part of. I think I will never have that, that is a loss, that is pain. But out of that loss has come a gain, it's because of that loss that I know now that I am in the condition of re-imagining myself. I can see the connection between me and the Aboriginal in Australia or the Japanese or wherever else. I can invent a world in my own head and on my stage, that's my gain, and I can be passionate about England and the fact that I will die here, it may not be home but this is where I will die, I will not live elsewhere. If I talk critically it is because I can see the potential of England being something different. That's my gain and that gain comes from the fact that I am all too aware of my loss. Now I think white England needs to face up to the fact of what is lost, there is no Empire, there is no centrality of the world, and through that one will appreciate what one has gained or is gaining.

No one can be blind to the change that over the last two decades has happened in the simplest area of all, which everyone kind of ignores but which is so vital – diet. What was the diet twenty years ago when you went out to eat and what's the diet now? Look at the range! Are we better or are we worse off? That gain comes from a sense of appreciating what one has lost. Okay, no problem, that's my condition as a modern person.

Q: Surely that is where integration takes place – within the individual. There is no question of immigration. It seems to me that there is no thing called black theatre unless it's defined, as you have done, in an English context. You didn't use the word British, in an English context. If you look at theatre in Nigeria or in India do you see black theatre? I'm interested in your word Binglish. I use a word Bigerian coming from Nigeria and Barbados and living in England. The integration happens within me, it does not necessarily happen in the outside world. Thus, from my definition of Bigerian Theatre, everything I do has an element of those things that make me.

A: But as you say yourself, it's only in this (English) context alone that our terms make any sense. One of the potentials we possess, manifested in much work over the years, has been a new kind of discourse, which is not just a discourse with England (in for example a negotiation with language or with form) but also a discourse with Africa and various parts of Asia. For example one takes a form and quotes from it. You think that you are doing it in a form of theatre which is from India or from Africa, but in fact it isn't. In the journey of that form from there to here, through the bodies of actors who are not Indian or African, it has changed. Now you could then say to yourself, 'Well I'm attempting to do a kind of Indian theatre,' but actually, you're not doing it. You can't possibly do it because you're not part of that culture, you're not part of that texture. Your texture is a mixture of your feelings about whatever space you're in and the culture that's forming. Now in that sense I think that black theatre is a kind of valid term, though I agree with virtually everyone who feels that it's not specific enough, which is why we come up with Bigerian, with Binglish; I mean those are really attempts to move forward in a kind of closer and closer definition of what is actually the sense of this particular type of theatre which can be shared across the spectrum of groups working in this context.

Q: Does the term black theatre give people preconceived ideas?

A: Certainly, but I don't think it necessarily means it should be dismissed without finding an adequate enough replacement. Because, the fact of the matter is, you can say well we're just a theatre company, but that won't work in pragmatic terms. That is simply to do with the fact of the ways in which venues perceive you, the ways in which the public perceives you and it is a reality of England now that we do see people in certain kinds of blocks. So I say, why fly against that reality, I'm fine with that, I have no great problem. So long as I can open one thing, that this is not a fixed entity. For example, from the beginning of when we started our group to about the mid 80's, my sense of Asia was quite specific, quite narrow, it was essentially people who in some way or the other were related to the Indian sub-continent be they Muslims or Hindus or Sikhs, be they directly from there, or indirectly from there, it didn't really matter. But from the mid 80's onwards I began to think, 'Now hang on a minute, I'm forced to acknowledge the fact that there's an increasing presence of Chinese here, and people from other parts of Asia, are they not Asian?" Literally, on the atlas, the continent of Asia stretches from what is considered Asia Minor, which is Turkey, right across to Japan. Why am I holding on to the term in this narrow sense? I had to reflect that that term emerged specifically. It's unique term which emerged here because of this mass exodus of Indians in the 1960s and they were immediately termed Asians because you just said Asians, right that's fine and everyone understood. The people who are less polite said 'Pakis' and even then everyone understood. But that term is expansive, there is constant evolution of it, and the one has to be aware that you don't stay fixed with a term and that there are other inclusions within it. As much as there are tensions within it. I used the term Paki a year ago in a workshop, I mean it's my kind of normal bent to use a term because it becomes a way of diffusing the situation, so I use it quite freely. A fourteen year old Asian student at the end of the workshop, asked 'Why did you say Paki?" So I of course went off into my political drivel ('Well you know this was the way in which people were using the term and I think it's great because it becomes a way in which the aggressor's term is atually used by yourself to undermine it'). He said, 'No you are not proud of yourself, why do you not then say Pakistani?' I suddenly realised, oh! my God, this generation has got a whole other sense of that term which I never had. These important experiences just keep on making you aware that no term is fixed and you should not stay fixed with it, you should see what kind of evolution you want. Now personally, I do not subscribe to that kid's definition and I have no truck with it, I will not subscribe to that, just as much as I will not subscribe to a sense which says, well black theatre is only for, or only means people from Africa, or Asia but does not include Chinese and so forth, I think that's wrong, that's my personal view.

Performing Arts International
1996, Vol. 1, Part 2, pp. 23–33
Reprints available directly from the publisher
Photocopying permitted by license only

© 1996 OPA (Overseas Publishers Association)
Amsterdam B.V. Published in The Netherlands
by Harwood Academic Publishers
Printed in India

Black Theatre Development at Theatre Royal, Stratford East

Philip Hedley

Artistic Director, Theatre Royal.

In his introduction, Leon Rubin spoke of Philip Hedley as a fighter and one who has stayed close to his community and his artistic vision, 'an artistic director other artistic directors look towards for inspiration'.

Through the 1980s and '90s, Philip Hedley, Artistic Director of Theatre Royal, Stratford East, has been crucially instrumental in recognising the distinctive qualities of culturally various theatres and the integrated nature of much black performance; he has encouraged new writing and given space to new developments. Productions at Theatre Royal continue to attract large and varied audiences and succeed in winning critical interest and attention. In the following paper, which is an edited version of a transcript, Philip Hedley identifies some of his own learning points as well as some particular approaches and ways of working that have contributed to making Theatre Royal significant in recent Black Theatre development.

I am talking to you as, originally, and to some extent still, a white racist, and I want you to know why I say such a thing and what I mean by it. I was born before the Second World War, so when I was in school we were shown all those classic stereotypical things. I can remember being shown the globe and the teacher had a spoon and showed how small England was beside the head of the spoon, then I was shown all the red areas on the map: 'See how important we are'. We were an entirely white class of course, and my own experience of black people was from Tarzan films on Saturday mornings: black people leaping up and down; black people being villainous; black people being servants, and all the rest of it, all those cliches you know about, and disgracefully those films are still shown. So that's where I was coming from. As I grew up in Manchester, after the war, I didn't see any black people; I may have seen the occasional American serviceman during the war, but I can't remember it. Then I went to Australia. I trust you know something of how, in the 1950s and '60s, Aboriginees were still excluded from white society, perhaps not so much now, though the battle continues. So my experience was not good for not being a racist, if you see what I mean. I had to go through a stage of seeing black people on television, speaking about politics or some other topic, and of thinking, 'Isn't that black person talking intelligently. How interesting.' I don't know how far I've got on that journey of learning about my own racism. It's hard isn't it, digging out things like that from yourself, especially when the impressions are given to you so young. I don't know if it is easy for young people present to know what it was like when there were very few black people in England, or at least where I was from. There's no doubt that those appalling depictions in Tarzan films do go into one's brain and have influence.

So my journey towards being asked to speak at a conference like this is a very long one. I still have a lot to learn and there are lots of things I'll never know about these issues, because I'm not black.

All I can talk about is where I am now, and where my theatre is now and what it has and has not achieved, and where it may get to, particularly in relation to black theatre.

My philosophy for Theatre Royal Stratford East, tied up with that of Joan Littlewood, who was there before me. Joan Littlewood was a re-markable director, hailed by the very establishment people she despises. Peter Hall has said that as far as he's concerned the two directors with real genius and innovation since the war are Joan Littlewood and Peter Brook, and Richard Eyre has said the same thing, but Joan is so completely against the establishment, it's a sort of rule of her life. I was absolutely with you, Jatinder, with what you were saying about English acting being from the neck up and that's actually what Joan

Left to right: A.J. India, Nitin Chandra Ganatra and Paul Sharma in *D'Yer Eat with Your Fingers?! – The Remix*, at Theatre Royal, Stratford East, directed by Indhu Rubasingham, 1995. Photograph by Richard H. Smith.

could have said forty years ago; her theatre was very physical and incorporated music and song. She won acclaim abroad first, it was the French who discovered her, then slowly the English began to acknowledge her work. Noel Coward said of her, 'She's an extraordinary woman, real touch of genius, but a total amateur'. That ties in again, Jatinder (Verma), with your identifying a need for a new critical judgement. The critical judgement wasn't there for assessing Joan fully in her time. Joan's theatre was a working class rebellion, a working class voice, which didn't otherwise exist in theatre at all that time. It was based on a very simple philosophy, which Joan used to call 'a continuous loop' between the community and the stage; you draw themes, ideas, talent, people from your community, you create theatre with them and give it back. There's a 'continuous loop' between drawing from your community, making a play from that material and reflecting it back.

Now one of the major reasons I've been fifteen years at Stratford East is because it's a working class district, which is natural for myself, and very mixed racially. It's now 43% Afro-Asian, and that is wonderful for

Shobna Gulati in *Moti Roti, Puttli Chunni*, at Theatre Royal, Stratford East, directed and designed by Keith Khan and Ali Zaidi 1993. Photograph by Alastair Muir.

the artistic director of a theatre. If you have the philosophy that you're serving your local community, drawing from it and giving back in that continuous process, with a mixed race community it's a tremendous plus because your work is very very varied. Now I'm not just going to tell the history of the last fifteen years. I hope I can make some points along the way, because it's an interesting process to review.

You would almost have thought I had three five-year plans over those fifteen years, but I can't claim that at all, it was just a natural development of hanging on to that philosophy. In the first five years there was a sprinkling of black work, the occasional invited show, a co-production of *Welcome Home Jacko* which was very successful. I was feeling my way. Gradually more black work came through, then more and more. In the first five years of my time there, when we produced a black play, it was usually in the bottom quarter of our box office, it was somewhere near the bottom, apart from a sudden huge leap in audience figures with *Welcome Home Jacko,* because most of the actors concerned were in a television series at the time called *No Problem.* Now, fifteen years later, if I was thinking strictly commercially, black theatre is almost the safest thing I could do, there's such demand for it. We had to persevere for some time so that word got about, until people realised how accessible our theatre was, and how cheap. Of the eight productions we will be doing this year, six will be black; I could begin to get complaints from the 56% white majority in our district soon, which won't worry me at all, I'll be very pleased when I start getting those complaints, if I do. It's gone that far because of natural development; I can't claim credit for it being thought out. How that process has taken place interests me and several things within that process. In the first ten years, the majority of work, which wasn't a great deal, consisted of white directors directing black plays. Now, however, by far the majority of black or Asian plays are black or Asian directed. There have only been two exceptions in the last four years: one was a co-production with the National Theatre and they'd chosen the director before I got there; the second case involved a writer with whom I have a particularly strong relationship over many years and it would seem foolish, for the sake of dogma, to break that relationship.

A further and natural part of this process is about how much black theatre work has been coming through at the moment. I was reading an interview with Norman Beaton, the senior black actor in this country, (in *Desmonds* on TV), where he said: 'The other thing that is changing, quite gloriously, is that when I go to see a play with this generation of young Afro-Caribbean people, there is an energy and a vibrancy that I hardly find on the white stage. They're bad, really, really bad, and that sort of energy must have the opportunity to be seen.' Well if you have that original philosophy of being in touch with your local community and its expressing itself to itself, then when you've got that kind of vibrancy and energy coming through from your local community, to a certain section of your community, then it's very easy to allow it to be expressed because you get bloody good shows on the stage through that process, shows which are as vibrant and energetic for a white audience as for a black audience. Beaton said a little later: 'Once you can get theatres to create space for young black directors, they will be able to take the discipline of stage craft and use that to bring out the best of their own performers to do the work written by their own people'. I certainly agree with that too.

Now in this process, as it developed at Stratford East, there was an interesting middle stage where I spotted a closed door in my own mind, to do with casting. Obviously there are specifically black/white parts in some modern plays where racism is the subject and you cast black and white accordingly. It would be foolish to move those over. But in other areas, and with the majority of directors in charge of theatres in this country, I believe it is still true that there are closed doors in peoples' brains about black casting and I noticed one in myself about seven or eight years ago. I did a production of a play about Josephine Baker, the wonderful black American performer who made it and became famous in France. In her life story she goes from a black childhood into a sort of white American theatre run by white people and then to a France where she met mostly whites and mixed mostly with white people. Casting a play where you're only allowed ten to twelve actors and where you're going to have black and white characters throughout, it seemed important how to use black or white actors in her story. I arranged auditions for one week for a lot of white and black actors and thought 'I'll have five black and five white and I can easily mix them up to tell the story,' but I realised after the first day of auditioning with the black actors, that a much better way of doing it was with an all-black cast. Then I got into that stupid sort of thinking, wondering how to indicate when an actor was playing white. I'm ashamed of that stupid thinking because when they were playing white, of course it came across to the audience, through their sense of period, place, how they spoke etc. Then I was casting the next play, a Victorian melodrama set in England, and pondering in the back of my mind, as you do when you're casting, about the part of the detective, which was a very flamboyant detective indeed: 'Who might be the right person to play that?' I was watching my own production of *The Josephine Baker Story* and was looking at Ben Thomas, who happened to be playing the hell-fire southern preacher, and I suddenly thought, 'That's the quality I want in the part of the detective'. Then I cross-questioned myself. Wasn't I thinking of casting white for that part, thinking historically? I'm very glad to say that I made the right connection, and at the end of the performance offered Ben Thomas the part.

There was that door, that block in my own mind about casting. It's interesting to me to reflect on how long it took me to discover it and sad that it took me so long to discover it in myself and to see its obviousness, and I'm afraid it's true that there are a lot of locked doors still in the minds of people running our theatres.

One of the most exciting things that has been happening at our theatre the last few years has been the group called The Posse, eight very talented, thirty-ish black actors, whom I've got to know well over the years, in some cases directing them in plays. Following two Sunday night 'variety shows' at our place, in which they were involved in doing sketches, they wrote me a letter saying: 'Will you give us the theatre for a Sunday night. We want to take the reins into our own hands,' that was the expression they used, I remember, 'We have no script, we don't know what we're going to do, but we want the theatre'. I said yes, and they concocted a review, a collection of sketches, and that went on to become more Sunday nights, a three week run, a tour of England. They played at ten theatres round England, really breaking barriers in terms of getting black audiences in. Earlier this year they did another version of that show; in three month's time they're going to do a third version, *The Posse* 3, and then there will be a big television series from it next year from all these sketches that they're getting together. What was interesting about that, was their taking the reins into their own hands; they wrote it themselves, they acted it, and most unusually and interestingly in terms of form, – and forget black for a moment – they directed it themselves: there were eight directors, eight actors, eight people marketing it, eight people producing it, eight people doing everything in it, and God, that was a stimulus to my own theatre. I was having to adapt to eight directors on a show.

They've been gloriously unashamed about learning. They want to know. They've gone on every course to do with being a Board member, to do with budgeting, to do with marketing, to do with writing; anything going, they're eating up experience, with great strength among themselves. Six months behind them was a women's group called The Bibi Crew, coming through exactly the same process, and this year there's an Asian group that has done a Sunday night and they are setting off on that same process too; there will be three of them buzzing round the country, touring, breaking barriers, teaching white administrators of theatres an awful lot about marketing and how you can get through in ways that are not boring. You know there are people sitting in offices devising strategies and then they send their brochure to the local library and think that's marketing. I actually got extra money for *The Posse* 3 from the Arts Council, for them to go to towns three months before the tour. They'd go into the black district, get their hair cut there, go to restaurants, go to discos wearing the Posse T-shirts the whole

Left to right: Suzanne Packer, Judith Jacob, Beverley Michaels and Josephine Melville in The Bibi Crew's production *On a Level*, at Theatre Royal, Stratford East, 1993. Photograph by Richard H. Smith.

Left to right: Michael Buffong, Robbie Gee, Gary McDonald, Eddie Nestor and Roger Griffith's in The Posse's production *Armed and Dangerous*, at Theatre Royal, Stratford East. Photograph by Johnny Munday.

time; they'd be giving out leaflets, dropping in on youth clubs, doing impromptu drama sessions, uninvited but instantly welcomed, and altogether marketing in a way that is a vastly more imaginative and active way than is ever normally done in theatre. Of course it's deeply unusual for you to be able to go out early before a tour and do that. Again, they met some closed minds. The marketing director from a Midlands theatre said to me: 'Extraordinary Philip, you know when you came with that early show that was black, we didn't get a very good audience, but when The Posse came, we did just the same things we always do in marketing. Wasn't it extraordinary the number of people that came!' I said, 'Well didn't the lads come up early, you know, two months before for three weeks and...'. 'Oh yes, yes, but we did exactly the same things we always do', and she wouldn't have it that that was marketing. Going out and talking to people, getting them involved, that wasn't marketing. You do that with shuffling bits of paper around.

So the writing is coming through and there are commissions for next year. It's been a slow process of trust and knowing the doors are open. Of the eight commissions I've got out for next year, six are black – I'm including Asian in that category. I was interested, Jatinder, in what you were saying about the black aesthetic and critical judgement of it. You'd think from what I'm saying that I was coming strictly from the social aspect, but I'm coming from that 'continuous loop' from which you create drama and art. The Posse, The Bibi Crew and the Asian group, – who haven't even got a name yet, they're so new, – are not breaking that much new ground in theatre, but it's the connection with the audience. Thirty odd years ago, when I was working in Newham, the poorest and most deprived borough in the whole of England, I took a party of about twenty seventeen year old engineering apprentices to the theatre. I was supposed to be teaching them English on Wednesday nights and the only way I could get them to write any English was to get them to write dirty jokes for the first six weeks till they realised they couldn't shock me. They were terrified of the theatre. These were lads who'd get off their bikes, climb through the window, drop into their desks and challenge me to teach them. I took them to the theatre and it was an extraordinary experience for them and for me. I was ten minutes later than I should have been to meet them at the theatre. I ran in and got the tickets, went through the foyer to the bar and back again and couldn't find them, went out the front and looked, did the foyer, the bar, went out the front again and I'd gone past them twice without recognising them, nor had they dared speak to me. They were in suits, white shirts, ties, dressed in a way I'd just never seen them, and they were frightened, all these tough lads, going to an elitist theatre, yes even out theatre to those of you who know it was to them a snob event, and yet afterwards, their constant refrain was, 'It's just like my mum and dad'. They couldn't get over the fact their life was on the stage, they couldn't believe that it connected in that way.

Now that's happened a lot over the last ten years with the black and Asian audiences, that hunger for the way drama tries to make sense of an incident or give shape to something, the way it puts people's lives on stage, even, sometimes, unfortunately in too stark a way. The first Asian play we commissioned was about racism in Southall, with white racists attacking Asians, and I remember the Guardian review said, 'Oh not another play about racism. Don't we know all this? Hasn't this been said before?' I had a meeting in the bar with a young Asian in the audience who introduced me to a black friend who'd not been to the theatre before, and exactly the incident from the play happened to them outside the theatre. They went into the precinct, they were attacked and they went to the police station. Amazingly, the police had caught their attackers, not for attacking them, but for attacking property earlier in the evening, and the police would not charge these young men with attacking the Asian and the black man, even though the black lad said, 'that's my blood on his shoulder.' And there's the Guardian saying

Zita Sattar (left) and Nina Wadia in *D'Yer Eat with Your Fingers?!* – *The Remix* produced at Theatre Royal, Stratfort East, directed by Indhu Rubasingham, 1995. Photograph by Richard H. Smith.

'Don't we know all about this? hasn't it been said before?' That was almost too close to the 'continuous loop' between your local community and what's going on on the stage.

Now strictly on the education side and going into schools, I've said to our education officer, 'Look the only thing worth dealing with in this borough is racism. We've got to find a million different ways of dealing with it'. We have the BNP in the south of the borough and we have five candidates standing in our borough with the title 'Conservatives against Labour's Ethnic Policies', a clearly racist stand, so to me that certainly is the only thing worth dealing with in schools. We are indeed invited in by teachers who say they find it difficult to deal with and that it's easier if the subject is raised by an outside team of actors doing a play about it. We took the situation of the murder of a young local Asian and made a play to do with the witnesses, people who must have seen what happened but didn't speak up; the kids cross-questioned the characters who were the witnessess and it led to some extremely lively discussions and exposure of racism in those classes; the kids' discussions amongst themselves were sometimes tough but they were extremely worthwhile.

Wilbert Johnson and Claudette Williams in *Running Dream* by Trish Cooke, directed by Olusola Oyeleye, at Theatre Royal, Stratford East, 1993. Photograph by Alastair Muir.

Meanwhile on the Theatre Royal stage, what we are doing is empowering more and more of the groups that are starting up with us. Groups like The Posse, The Bibi Crew and the Asian Group have already set up as production companies and have complete charge. Audiences sense that this is themselves in charge, and saying what they want to say, and they have an invigorating, exciting night out. The white members of the audience have a good night out as well because they sense something going on; they may not understand all of it, but they have a bloody good night out. Through people being in charge of their own work you get the best excitement for all members of the audience, because there's something real happening between stage and audience. You can't have theatre without the audience. Theatre exists in the process between stage and audience. The more exciting it is on stage, and the more varied your audience are in age, race, class and every possible way, the more resonance there is for what's happening on stage, there are more pockets of laughter going on and people unconsciously negotiating off each other. Audiences unconsciously become a group during the evening, and the wider the resonance, the more you're negotiating and the wider your experience becomes. The mix of the audience is important for the theatre event. I don't understand why people don't recognise why that mixture is so worth aiming for. I did a play by Tunde Ikole called *Scrape off the Black*. The central character has a black father and a white mother who has gone with black men all her life but talks racism all the time. There'd be laughter in the audience from some sections and 'Aaahhh! You can't say that', from the others, and as the white liberals began to realise 'Just a minute, who's laughing at these jokes? oh it's black people, I see, and what are we white liberals allowed to laugh at in this context?' so they sorted themselves out through the evening. They all had a bloody good night out ultimately, because they really went through a process in relation to what was going on on the stage. What more can you ask?

Performing Arts International
1996, Vol. 1, Part 2, pp. 35–41
Reprints available directly from the publisher
Photocopying permitted by license only

Arts Education and Cultural Diversity

Maggie Semple

Head of education at the Arts Council of England. She headed the imaginative and productive AEMS project (the Arts Education for Multicultural Society project) at the Arts Council and has extensive knowledge and experience of both the arts scene in Britain and educational developments. Her own background is in dance performance. She has a proven record of awakening interest in people to arts experience across cultural boundaries.

Introduction

The arts are the intangible soul of society. Through unreconstructed histories they connect with imaginations of the past and propel us into the future. Knowing the arts, provides us with a legacy and a sense of hope.

A wise griot, summing up his message for an audience reminded them of the saying: 'One hand cannot clap'. A young boy laughed out loud at this, shouting, 'Of course one hand can clap, but it needs the assistance of another'. The griot turned slowly and smiled. He surveyed the hushed audience and paused on the two shining eyes of the impetuous speaker. 'You are right, my young friend, when a hand of one and the hand of another meet, they signify respect and harmony. It is when only one hand is portrayed and only one part of a message told, that we see a limited view of reality'.

My own work in researching, talking about and writing about the arts is concerned centrally with arts education and cultural diversity, the one hand meeting another in sustained applause.

Like the griot I often find myself in the position of storyteller, relating the experiences of artists in schools and colleges to teachers and educationalists, for stories are a way to make personal and communal meaning out of human experience.

Arts in Society at Odds with the Political Agenda

The arts have always led a precarious existence in society. They can subvert, persuade, seduce, startle and reflect attitudes and behaviour and have the ability to challenge or maintain the status quo. The arts can act as powerful agents and often live a dual existence, at times, conforming to, and at other times opposing, the dominant aesthetic.

Currently there is a unique relationship between Arts in Society and Arts Education, in that both have been subjected to intense scrutiny by a political ideology which has redefined their function. Arts in Society has attempted to legitimize its role by proving that the arts are a viable economic industry. The arts earn more annually than the motor industry. As a generic area of the curriculum, Arts Education seems to be at odds with the political agenda; education legislation reveals little influence from decades of debate and policy-making by arts educators and it could be argued that by naming a few of the arts, but not all, the National Curriculum has established a hierarchy between them. As someone acting on the dance lobby, I know how painful it is to have dance placed within P.E., for instance.

Arts in Society and Arts Education are united in both being open to influence from arts outside the European tradition. Factions arise from divided interests and the subsequent allocation of resources, from debate over what is worth funding and teaching and by whose criteria such judgements should be made. I would argue that works of art are created, and should therefore be interpreted, within a social context; they are expressions of creativity in time, place, culture and technology.

At the same time, there are also examples of well-established 'intercultural' ideas which have been widely adopted without there being a need to refer to their cultural origin. R.C. Kwant, addressing *The International Association for Intercultural Education*, in Bergen in 1987, suggested the example of Arabic numerals.

> Initially we counted with the help of words, but at a certain level words became insufficient: we invented other symbols which we called numbers. We learned to 'operate' with numbers. There are many different systems of numbers. The Hebrew, Greek and Latin systems made use of some of the letters of their alphabets. The Arabs invented a new, simple and effective system, using numbers 1 to 9 with 0. Operations which were difficult in preceding systems, like multiplying in Roman numerals, become easy. ...This system has been invented within a particular culture, but it is so clear, so rational, that it has been adopted by other cultures and now is accepted all over the world. It can be called an 'intercultural reality'.

This 'intercultural reality' is adopted by cultures without having to enter into Arabic culture to understand it. It maintains its own identity and is not weakened if we forget its origin. However, Kwant goes on to point out that artistic expression is not intercultural in this sense because it is thoroughly rooted in a particular culture.

There is an immense difference between an 'intercultural object', like the Arabic system of numerals, and an 'artistic expression'. Both are cultural creations, but the first is loosened from its individual and cultural roots to become a formal system. An 'artistic expression', however, remains connected with personal and cultural roots. The maker remains recognizable in it, and it bears the stamp of the culture in which it came into existence.

Artistic expression does not present a world of final solutions. It stresses the problems and unmasks solutions. In this way it brings cultures nearer to each other, not as finally united but as scenarios of similar ambivalence and struggle.

If we are searching for examples of how we might analyse cultures, Umberto Eco's essay *Innovation and Repetition* (1985), which deals with seriality and modern aesthetic theory can provide a discussion point. He indicates how, in classical periods, novelty was not given a high status and the differences between so-called major and minor arts were not stressed. He offers a typology of different kinds of repetition in the arts, which I paraphrase as follows:

The Retake – Here characters are used from a previous adventure but we are shown what happens to them after the first adventure has ended. Examples are *Star Wars* and *Superman,* in which familiar characters are engaged in new adventures.

The Remake – The retelling of a story. Shakespeare remade preceding stories, demonstrating that it is possible to remake without repeating. Interestingly, Broadway musicals invariably have a plot which is a remake of a novel.

The Series – involves familiar characters around whom secondary characters revolve to generate the sense that new stories are created. In truth, the narrative scheme does not change substantially. We enjoy the novelty of difference in the stories and gain the pleasure of familiarity with a narrative that really is not different. The Sunday evening heroics of Hercule Poirot spring to mind, or the films of actors like John Wayne who seem to make the same films over and over again.

The Saga – Sagas involve the activities of a family over time. In sagas people age and evolve. Sagas are disguised series, as in *Dallas*. They also seem to have the power to carry the same audience from one weekly episode to another.

Umberto Eco also shows that many works in literature, the arts and the mass media are continually quoting from other works that preceded them. The arts are full of parodies, plagiarisms, retakes, remakes and ironic intertextual jokes, all of which, Eco argues, suggests that at the moment we have returned to an aesthetic based on similarity and unity, not difference and diversity.

This presents us with particular problems in making a positive approach to cultural difference. As Raymond Williams in *Keywords* (1983) points out: 'Culture' is a complex term that carries particular meanings in different disciplines. I would add that our definition of culture too has particular resonance for us as artists, and it lies at the roots of our educational practice.

Peter Abbs has suggested two views of historic culture: the conservative and the postmodern. In the conservative, the cultural continuum offers us work which challenges, educates and expands us – it is our inheritance; whereas, the postmodern offers material to be endlessly refashioned, raided, rectified, reformulated – it is our eclectic workshop.

Cultural values, beliefs and symbols of a group (its *representations*) are produced and shared collectively by those who are the members of the group. Like a language, they are not produced by individuals as a result of their own cultural initiative. Indeed, individuals who produce their own values, beliefs and symbol systems are frequently ostracised by others, treated with hostility, regarded as mad, or tolerated as interesting eccentrics. In any case they are not treated as full members of the group, precisely because they do not share its cultural meanings. Those of us who are artists, will have personal experience of this at some point in our creative lives.

National Curriculum and National Culture

Education and culture have always been closely related. Education reflects the dominant values of society and at the same time is the vehicle for transmitting them. Eric Bolton, former Chief HMI, posed the question, 'is it possible for a public education service to have a different culture or set of dominant values from the society it serves?'

The cultural question is how to make meaningful diversity rather than just a collection of fragments. The question is too hot because cultural policy means asserting one version of the national past and by implication one version of the national present. In launching the working group on History, Kenneth Baker, then Secretary of State, said, 'the programmes of study should have at their core the history of Britain, the record of its past and in particular, it is a political, constitutional and cultural heritage'. Despite recent trends in teaching history, there have been concerted efforts to deny approaches recognising the multiplicity and provisional nature of perspectives in favour of an authoritative (and authoritarian) emphasis on 'the facts'.

Dawn Gill (1990) has pointed out that, even in the working group's final report, of the 31 named individuals who were suggested for compulsory study, only two were women and all were Europeans. It is therefore evident that, far from promoting an equality of experience, subject positions and role models open to girls and black pupils confirm existing patterns of domination. Others claim that an apparent broadening of opportunity is in fact a reinterpretation, dilution and putting into forms which support or do not contradict other elements within the dominant culture. Insisting that all girls study science up to the age of 16 might, for example, help to counter long-standing under-representation of women in the physical sciences. However, merely to make the high status curriculum available to all pupils, without reference to the cultural resources they bring to it, is likely to favour the already privileged.

In many ways, the National Curriculum created by the Education Reform Act reflects nostalgia for a national 'past' as much as it does a concern with modernization. Its proponents have been called, 'cultural restorationists' (Ball, S. 1990).

Education for Integrity

While multicultural/anti-racist education has a history of documentation, there has been little recording and debate of an arts philosophy which reflects an understanding of cultural diversity. Some teachers have responded to the challenge of the National Curriculum by conducting their own internal arts audit which has enabled them to re-examine their curricular content and practice. It is simple enough to understand that drawing from a fixed point of observation produces one kind of a picture with one perspective and therefore one way of depicting reality. A multi-cultural/anti-racist arts curriculum rejects this singular view and begins by acknowledging that Britain has always been a culturally diverse society.

A Perceived Cultural Hierarchy

Responses to the arts reflect values, ideas and beliefs and in Britain there is a perceived hierarchy rooted in the critical values and aesthetic understanding of Western European art forms. This is the dominant aesthetic, a notion I would like to examine more closely in a moment, held to be the pinnacle of artistic achievement and, consequently, placing non-European art in opposition to it. This perceived hierarchy is also perpetuated in Arts Education, (despite the effective work of practitioners). For example it can be found in the study programmes of initial teacher training courses, specialist colleges of dance, music, drama and visual arts, as well as in 'A' level courses and, inevitably, in the National Curriculum.

In the Western tradition, 'being creative' is too often thought to be a personal talent, not arising from a creator's circumstance but a private ownership of ideas, viewed as property on sale to the highest bidder. The perceived hierarchy and such inflexible notions of creativity have led to the Eurocentric 'grand narrative' being presented as if it were universal.

Whose Arts?

While many teachers willingly reappraise their content and delivery to ensure a culturally balanced arts curriculum the dilemma is often *whose* arts should be presented? It is important that we answer this question with regard to establishing cultural pluralism, rather than with reference only to the pupils and students of a particlar school or college.

The arts play an important part in establishing and maintaining an individual's sense of cultural identity. However all cultures are dynamic and organic, evolving and changing in response to outside influences. There is a need to be sensitive to the competing and sometimes conflicting tensions between cultural conservation and cultural development and synthesis. These two notions, however, need not be mutually exclusive. At its most crude, a culturally balanced curriculum would not consist of a lesson on Africa one week followed by India the next, but would present a broad and heterogenous curriculum which draws positive advantage from different cultural traditions. What I propose is a constantly shifting file of cultural languages and ideas, relating one to another, sometimes complementarily and sometime oppositionally, in a dialectic of dissonance and convergence that allows no single term either monopoly or domination.

Marie-Francoise Chavanne (1986) stresses three aspects in *Many Cultures: Many Arts*:

– the plural, which guarantees multiplicity and diversity, and assures us of a broad view without hierarchical ordering of cultures or arts.
– interactions between arts and cultures – the phenomena of osmosis and cultural contacts have for centuries accompanied the life of civilisations.
– permanent evolution of culture and arts, which bear witness to the past but which remain perpetually active and in constant development.

Arts in Daily Life: Orature

Many artists from outside the European tradition view the arts as inseparable from daily life. The physical, cultural, social, psychological, economic and political dimensions of society are all bound up with the arts. Consequently when non-European artefacts are placed within a European context they are often seen as exotic.

Arts which are inseparable from daily life produce artefacts that are not only functional but also symbolic of complex relationships within the society. This understanding is called 'orature', in which the main thrust resists and challenges the trend towards seeing art as purely decorative. Orature includes the structures, aesthetics, process of creativity, values and traditions of a society; the most important 'actors', 'poets', 'painters' and so on are the people. It is within this view of arts production that black artists legitimise their role within arts education.

Artists are aware that not only do they bring a different perspective into an educational establishment, but also they present a different methodology. Most artists believe that orature is at its best when it operates within a democratic structure of creativity. This means that the approach is non-didactic, without marked distinction between expert and non-expert. At the same time it is not learner-centred, which would be problematic where a student is locked into racist views or behaviour which will need to alter. The mode is collaborative, group-centred learning. The production of the work is as important as the work itself in that the origin of the materials and how they are used are themselves essential issues for debate.

Many black artists come from societies which have been culturally diverse for centuries, and are well placed to enhance education in England. For many teachers, the artists' ability to work comfortably in a cross-curricular way is seen as unusual, but for the artists their work is of its nature multi-faceted, as well as already reflecting cultural diversity.

Teachers and artists ensure a context in which non-Western art does not appear quaint, primitive, confused or unworthy of serious critical attention. They are storytellers in the time-honoured tradition, who remind us of our responsibilities, our special gifts, our right place in the interplay of ideas. We are embarked on a journey through different aesthetics, where races and genders and spiritual beliefs are mixed, boundaries are broken. I believe this produces a new stronger aesthetic, with the concept of creativity informed by relationship, harmony, balance and dignity.

Performing Arts International
1996, Vol. 1, Part 2, pp. 43–48
Reprints available directly from the publisher
Photocopying permitted by license only

Panel: Present Practice Bringing Students and Live Theatre Together

Sita Brahmachari

As Education Officer at Talawa Theatre Company, she has created a network of interest in black theatre through her text workshops in schools and colleges, and through Talawa's workshop and dramaturg programmes provides support and development for theatre practitioners and writers.

At Talawa Theatre Company, at which I am Education Officer, we did a production of *King Lear*, and we had an interesting response from the newspaper critics. One critic wrote: 'One of the least endearing features of Talawa's *King Lear* is its flirtation with Afro-Caribbean culture, which becomes a dabbling in the exotic, even the primitive. Alas, poor Lear, we thought we knew him well'. Talawa's director, Yvonne Brewster, was amused at the suggestion that she could be accused of flirting with her own cultural heritage, but Yvonne took the critic's plaintive comment 'Alas, poor Lear, we thought we knew him well' as a compliment. There would be no point in any director or company putting on a production if all they intended to do was provide people with what they already knew. It's been interesting for me to measure the criticism against the unprecedented response we've had from student audiences in Secondary and Higher Education, many of whom, unlike our critic, do not know *Lear* well yet have been inspired to study, research and perform the play in colleges and schools. I'm reminded of the story of the renovation of the Sistine Chapel. Michelangelo's fresco had been covered over with dust for many years. When it was cleaned and restored many of the critics were horrified to discover the original and its brightness. My reply is "Alas, poor Michelangelo, we thought we knew you well!"

Through bringing students in contact with the work of a black theatre company, we aim to reinterpret the classics, and introduce modern classics by important black writers in Britain and throughout the world. In addition to producing classics such as *Lear*, *The Road* by Wole Soyinka,

43

The Importance of Being Earnest by Wilde, we also produce contemporary classics such as *The Love Space Demands* by African-American writer Ntozake Shange, and *Resurrections* by Nigerian writer Biyi-Bandele Thomas. By drawing upon a vast range of world theatre traditions we inevitably aim to broaden the perceptions of what theatre is, and to extend the cultural map, and so provide our audiences with a dynamic theatre of tradition. For Talawa this is not just an aim; our survival, and I would suggest, the survival of many other theatres in Britain, depends on securing the audiences of the future. The demographic profile of the future may surprise you. A London Weekend Television survey revealed that 'By the year 2000, 25% of people in Greater London between the ages of 18–25 will be from the so called ethnic minorities'.

In bringing students in contact with the work of a black theatre company we provide the stimulus for black students in particular to consider pursuing careers in theatre, and to enter Higher Education; moreover, we also provide productions of plays by black writers, and information on Talawa activities for all students across the educational spectrum.

Since our move to The Cochrane Theatre in 1991 we've received over 450 requests for information, ranging from students writing dissertations, requests for interviews with theatre practitioners, through to trainee teachers and actors wanting lists of plays by black writers. To cater for this demand we started holding seminars, so that students in higher education can actually speak to black writers, directors and performers and find out where best to train. A lot of these students who come to us are aspiring practitioners, haven't been in Higher Education, and are in their thirties or forties. If you attended one of our seminars the group might be made up of women of thirty years upwards.

I would like to discuss some student responses to our productions which point up the need for a real dialogue between students and black theatre practitioners. Their comments also reveal some of the difficulties we still face. The following is a comment from a secondary school student after attending Talawa's Production and Education Programme on *Antony and Cleopatra*. The Education Programme included a visit to Egyptology exhibition at the British Museum, followed by the Talawa production. The student said,

I've been studying Antony and Cleopatra for my GCSE exam all term. Before I came to your production I never really thought of the play as being set in Africa. The exhibition at the British Museum and your play has completely changed the way I look at the characters, especially Cleopatra as I didn't realise she was an African Queen.

To clarify that in someone's mind is an interesting achievement.

The joy of theatre to me is that it's live, it happens in the moment, but it's also a problem for black theatre practitioners because there are so few

Mona Hammond as The Fool in Talawa Theatre Company's production of Shakespeare's *King Lear*, 1994. Photograph by Richard H. Smith.

materials about the work of black theatre companies available in libraries or in recordings. To counteract this Talawa generally holds collaborative education projects. Although the majority of Talawa plays have a run of five weeks, through collaborative projects we are able to ensure that work can continue over the period of a term. We've repeated the format for three Talawa productions. For our first play at the Cochrane, *The Road* by Wole Soyinka, we collaborated with the Horniman Museum in South London, who had a year long exhibition on West African Yoruba art, religion and culture. And our *King Lear* has been photographically recorded by the Theatre Museum for an exhibition comparing Talawa's *King Lear* and The Royal Shakespeare Company's *King Lear*. We aim to make every production a lasting resource for teachers and students to draw on long after the production has finished.

A trainee teacher attended the Education Program for Soyinka's *The Road* and commented,

Before we came to the Yoruba exhibition and production I was worried about having to teach a lesson based on the play because I didn't know anything about African culture. As

Ben Thomas as Lear in Talawa Theatre Company's production of Shakespeare's *King Lear*, 1994. Photograph by Richard H. Smith.

a teacher I wouldn't think about teaching Shakespeare without telling students about the Elizabethan theatre, but what could I tell students about African theatre? I know it's not good enough as a teacher to say I wouldn't feel confident about teaching this play, but I feel at a disadvantage because I didn't learn anything about it at school or college. But the fact is that I've been studying Shakespeare for years and I've only just met Soyinka. Why?

This raises some important issues which, as teachers, we're constantly trying to address.

The increasing pressures that secondary school teachers face to deliver what is, in my view, a narrowing curriculum, would seem to make it even less likely in the future that students will go into higher education with knowledge of a writer like Soyinka. Indeed, if it wasn't for teachers being aware of the importance of offering their students a representative range of theatre experience, a student digesting recent theatre anthologies might well leave school with the impression that the number of black writers of stature throughout the world, let alone England, can be counted on the fingers of one hand. However, many secondary school and higher education students did attend the Production and Education Program and so had the experience of a live performance of a work by a Nobel Prize winning author who they might not otherwise have experienced (Soyinka's plays are very rarely produced in this country).

If it wasn't for such live performances and the determination of many teachers to find a way of delivering a representative curriculum, then black students in particular would leave school thinking that they had little to contribute to a theatre and literature tradition that fails to acknowledge our existence.

I just want to share with you an experience I recently had in a London school. A teacher wanted to bring students to our production *From the Mississipi Delta*, but (increasingly this happens) she couldn't get her students off their schedule. So she put up a poster of the production inviting students to an evening performance and left it for students to reply by signing up for themselves. She gave me a call and said, 'Could you come along to do a workshop because we have twenty students here who are interested'. So I went to this group and it was a group of black girls doing GCSE exams, and I did the workshop which worked out well for they also came to the production. As I walked through the school I realised that the school was predominantly white, so I asked the teacher 'Did none of the white students sign up?' She replied that 'No, nobody even requested any information about it'. Although I was very pleased that the black students had the rare opportunity to take part in the workshop I was saddened that there was not a single request by a white student to take part in the workshop or theatre visit. The seeds that the play was something too different, something that didn't concern them had already been planted. If such students then go into higher education they will carry the view that the work of a black theatre company is something extra-curricular, something that does not belong to the canon of work contributing to the evolution of English theatre.

To help to counteract this process Talawa set up its Education Program to make long term links across the education spectrum, from schools to universities. Through this program students are invited to attend a minimum of four productions. Each production is accompanied by a varied program of activities ranging from careers talks, to workshops with, for example, directors, choreographers, designers and so on. The result is that Talawa productions are programmed into the syllabus at GCSE level, A levels, BTEC, and degree level. This program encourages students to build up their own critical perspectives.

Students who have taken part in the Longterm Linkup Program have been able to employ some of the performance skills used in Talawa productions to create their own. Following a visit to Talawa's production of *The Love Space Demands* (which fused poetry, music and choreography), the A level and BTEC students wrote and presented their own choreopoems and were introduced to a new form of theatre. The majority of students attending Talawa skills workshops are from drama colleges. They are thus able to explore different approaches to performance.

For Talawa, school audiences are the mainstream audiences and the practitioners of the future. Through educational projects, such as collaborations and long term linkups, we aim to inspire those audiences and practitioners. We can do this by providing work that is evidence of the role of black theatre in the evolution of British theatre. If Talawa, along with many other theatres, do not achieve this we may find ourselves playing to empty houses.

Performing Arts International
1996, Vol. 1, Part 2, pp. 49–52
Reprints available directly from the publisher
Photocopying permitted by license only

Panel: Present Practice
A Personal Perspective on
Working in Theatre

Adjoa Andoh

Artistic Director and actor with Wild Iris Theatre Company, of which she is co-founder. She has wide experience of performing on stage and in film, television and radio, in both classic and innovatory work.

I set up a theatre company called *Wild Iris* with my friend Polly Irvine three years ago. There can be a romantic myth about being an actor and what a wonderful life it is. I think it's a terrible profession. I think it's full of neurotic, paranoid, unemployed people; yet frequently very gifted and frequently very frustrated, and I don't think anybody who's in-volved with the profession takes that lightly because we sort of know that that is what is going to happen to a lot of us a lot of the time. If you're a black actor you can multiply those difficulties by ten. Our position in the world, in this country, for all of us black people, has still not reached its full potential, and that is reflected in the acting profession.

For instance, I work in a BBC sitcom. I am the one black regular character in the show set in a hospital. I've heard the usual questions about 'Well, you're a nurse, but isn't that quite stereotypical?', or alternatively 'Why aren't there more of you because the nursing profes-sion is full of black women?'. There are black and Asian women and men who are doctors of all sorts, and who work in all areas of the health profession. We are there and yet we are not in this sitcom.

Neither are we in the audiences. We record the episodes in front of a live audience, and there are often only about five black people in an audience of 200 or so. I'll say afterwards 'Why haven't we got any black people here?' and people will answer 'Don't know really.' I say 'Well there are lots of black people involved in the health industry and they may for example find the jokes in the show funny.' The BBC put an advert in the black newspaper *The Voice* and within two weeks we had loads of black people coming along and being a brilliant audience, because black people are a brilliant audience; and it was so easy, all we had to do was say that we were doing this, it's on national television, and it's for you, so come and see it if you fancy it, or don't if you don't want to.

I think there's a way in which we are still excluded from the mainstream, and that's the same for me as an actor. I was having a driving lesson with my driving instructor, who's black and whose parents were Jamaican and he said 'Well, do you think we've got a chip on our shoulder? I mean are we always going on about how this has happened and that's happened because we're black, or is that just us making excuses?' I said 'Well no, I think that sometimes we all make excuses about things, but there are a lot of genuine concerns, and things that happen that are to do with being black are still going on in this society, which we're not really allowed to be part of yet'. He said he would really like to direct a film, and I told him he was mad because he'd make lots more in being a driving instructor. He told me that he wanted to direct a story about a Jamaican guy who's black, of English/Jamaican parents, and who goes to Jamaica thinking it's going to be going home, and it's going to be a wonderful life. He gets 'home' and he realises that he's in fact English, and that he doesn't actually fit-in in the ideal, comfortable way he thought he would. So, we ended up agreeing that our identities, though we have all sorts of things from everywhere else, are made of where we live in a day to day way, and that must be reflected in the work we see, the work we do, where we go (that we do go to see BBC sitcoms because we are here, and we pay our television licenses, so we should go), and where we should be able to go. Then why are football and cricket more important to lots of people than theatre? Because there's something live and dynamic and exciting there, and that is what our theatre should be. It has to touch people.

Our theatre company did a Restoration comedy written by a English white woman in 1700. It had been produced only four times. We did it with a mixed race cast and we stuck our poster in black cultural centres and all over the place. Publicity that says 'this is for you come and see it' is important. We got a black audience to come and see a Restoration comedy by a woman no one has ever heard of. They came and saw it and laughed and enjoyed it. It's a really good story all about what these men are doing to these women, and the women get together and say 'what did he say to you? Okay what are we going to do about him, girls'. It was well acted, everyone looked beautiful and wonderful and capable. It was an exciting event. Why shouldn't we do a Restoration comedy? Why shouldn't that be interesting? Why shouldn't that have resonances in our lives? Why shouldn't this happen?

I was acting in Derek Walcott's *The Odyssey* with the Royal Shakespeare company. Derek Walcott, from St Lucia, had just won the

Nobel prize. I went out on stage and every night I would see in an audience of 300, a smattering of black faces. Why? Do the RSC put posters up in Brixton, in Tottenham, do they advertise on black radio stations, do they advertise in *The Voice* newspaper? Sometimes I would stand on stage and I would just look and think 'well later for you'. I'm not criticising those who actually came and saw the play. There is a mailing list, there are people who buy tickets on a regular basis from the RSC, and it is they who will get first choice. *The Odyssey* was sold out even before it opened in London. I know loads of black people who wanted to come and see that play, because it's Derek Walcott, Derek Walcott at the RSC, it's a good play. Many people wanted to see it. They could not get a ticket because they're not on the mailing list. The thought pattern hasn't gone so far as to say 'actually, England is this big, and all these people pay tax to fund the RSC to do plays that are supposed to be for the nation'. Sometimes I wanted to take people from the administration at the RSC into my local Brixton pub and say 'now sit here and tell these people what their money has bought them this year, in what way you want them to attend the theatre, in what way you cater for them'.

It seems so straightforward and simple to me. I live here, we live here, we work here, we pay our taxes here, we want to have fun here. Black people go out, black people spend money, black people enjoy themselves. They should have access to enjoying all the areas that there are in this country. That's why I set up a theatre company, with my friend who is white. Everything is mixed: mixed genders, mixed races and so on. The theatre we're trying to create is one that is interesting and dynamic. I am interested in Lecoq, a French practitioner, whose work is intense and can cause actors to have rows and nervous breakdowns. I would like to have that in our work. I want to have a place where I can try to do that. I don't see why we shouldn't have that.

I did a soap opera on radio. My character was a stereotype of the dynamic black woman, with all the gear and the portable phone. She's beautiful and she's sexy. All the men are going 'Oh my god'. Taxi drivers would say to me 'You're a lot shorter than you are on radio'! One month we got scripts (by this stage we didn't have black writers writing for the show very often, in fact there were none in the two and a half years I was there, nor any black directors) in which they didn't know what to do with my character after she had screamed and shouted and bossed people about a bit, and had made lots of important phonecalls and faxes, and had driven a car around a bit which had made all the local men turn to jelly, and as they did not really know what to do with her it got to the stage where she worked for a gangster character. She had stopped working for herself and was now working for this gangster! The writers decided that one night my character gets very pissed and takes all her clothes off and asks the man to fuck her. And this was to go on over eight episodes on national radio. I thought I cannot do this. I cannot be the only black woman in this program and have to do this. I cannot do this just because they have run out of ideas. I read the scripts and cried. I realised I did not want black people to be listening to me having to do this. I talked to my friend and asked her if I was being a hysterical actress. She said she thought I was right in how I felt. I went to the producer, and without fuss, went through the script pointing out the problems. I felt it was implied that I had a chip on my shoulder and was being difficult. It's just a story, it's your character, there's an interesting character dynamic: that is how the writers felt. So we argued. Back and forth. It was really embarrassing, and as an actor I thought I would never work at the BBC again because I was being seen as being difficult. So I went to the other actors and, with their support, parts of the script were changed. It was not all changed but at least it wasn't as appalling as it could have been. For a good six months after that I felt I was carrying this reputation that I was difficult. I was not being difficult. I don't see why we cannot create work without having constantly to say 'let me in and hear what I'm saying, I'm not being difficult, I am a part of this'. That should be fine. Thus, this is partly why I set up my own theatre company.

Performing Arts International
1996, Vol. 1, Part 2, pp. 53–55
Reprints available directly from the publisher
Photocopying permitted by license only

Panel: Present Practice Trends in Black Writing for Theatre

Joan-Ann Maynard: Director

Joan-Ann Maynard has substantial experience of producing black theatre and of taking it to audiences across Britain. She has been Artistic Director of the highly-respected Black Theatre Co-Op and is Chair of the Black Theatre Forum.

Black Theatre Co-Op has a fifteen year history of producing plays, plays which present life from a black perspective, explore issues of relevance to the black community, extend language, explore dramatic styles and entertain a wider audience.

Because of the collaborative nature of theatre, and the wide range of skills involved in the theatrical process, viz music, choreography, set design, lighting, plus the skills of a director working with actors willing to explore, culturally, physically and mentally, this invariably involves the exposition on stage of a black aesthetic, an attempt to grapple with some indefinable element identified as black life, a black style, which years ago was identified as negritude. When choosing a text for production I am acutely aware of this legacy, and therefore try to bear in mind that I have some responsibility to embrace and extend this striving towards a full expression.

George Bernard Shaw had some eccentric things to say about theatre, especially about Shakespeare, but he also had a sound piece of advice when he visited Jamaica in 1911.

You want... a theatre, with all the ordinary travelling companies from England and America sternly kept out of it; for unless you do your own acting, and write your own plays, your theatre will be no use; it will, in fact vulgarise and degrade you.

Sound advice from an Irishman, not that black theatre practitioners needed Shaw to articulate a truth that was known instinctively.

BTC grew out of the need to create an authentic black theatre, the common beginning for most black theatre companies. The conditions for the emergence of a black aesthetic are created when Black playwrights, directors, actors and technicians honestly explore, mentally and physically, the boundaries of their art.

When choosing a play I find it very difficult to apply hard and fast rules; sometimes something indefinable attracts me to a text. But generally, I take a number of things into account. Will the play be dramatic? Most people would agree that a text becomes a play after it has been brought to life by production. Many scripts, although they read well, may in fact play badly. To be dramatic a text must deal with human problems and conflict, which can be seen, heard and felt by the audience.

I also look at the issues the text explores. Are these challenging to an audience? Will they have some lasting value and add meaning to the lives of the audience? The text should be able to engage, entertain and stimulate an audience. Are there issues of relevance to the black experience, and will the play have the capacity to strike a deep chord with black audiences, while at the same time have a universality?

I also take into account the language, and how the writer uses this basic tool, the writer's individuality. A play should possess distinctive characteristics. I look at the overall style of the piece, and try to identify the writer's original voice. Plays of interest, for me, explore novel ideas and look at situations in an innovative way.

Finally, I speculate on how the play is likely to be received by an audience. My choice of play is guided by my concern as both a producer and director, of how the play will work as a production, and the interest and audience it is likely to attract. These are likely to be a different set of criteria from those of an institution using the text for study instead of production.

The existence of a far flung black diaspora affords us a choice of material from Africa, North America, Latin America, the Caribbean and Britain. Some writers like Derek Walcott, and Wole Soyinka need no introduction. Nor in fact do a number of black American writers, such as James Baldwin, Lorraine Hansbury, Ed Bullins, Douglas Turner Ward and Langston Hughes, to name but a few. A number of contemporary American texts have been produced in Britain. *Nevis Mountain Dew*, *Eden*, and *Pecong*, by Steve Carter, *Fences* and *The Piano Lesson* by August Wilson, and works by George C Wolfe, Allison West, Ntozake Shange and Lonne Elder III, and there still remains a large untapped pool of black American plays. British audiences are also familiar with the works of Trevor Rhone, Dennis Scott, Earl Lovelace and Errol John, amongst others, from the Carribean.

Unlike the American and Caribbean situation, the selection of a play for production by a black British writer is problematic, because of the unavailability of text, even of plays that have received critical acclaim. There is no natural progression from production to text as is often the case with plays by mainstream white playwrights, though this may be primarily due to market forces. In spite of this however, texts can be found by writers such as Mustapha Matura, Hanif Kureshi, Caryl Phillips, Edgar White and Michael Ellis and other writers like Jackie Kay, Meera Syal, Trish Cooke and Zindika can be found in anthologies.

Our policy at BTC is to encourage new plays by black British writers, and this together with the work of other black companies, and sympathetic white institutions, should in time help to increase the volume of works that can be drawn upon.

When we come to consider the qualities and themes emerging in black British text I find that one recurring theme is the conflict between the older Caribbean born generation and the new British born generation, and their conflicting strategies for survival in an often hostile environment. Lorraine Hansbury's *A Raisin in the Sun* is the classic American example of this. British examples include *The Nine Night* by Edgar White, *Where There is Darkness* by Cas Phillips, *Paper and Stone* by Zindika and *A Hero's Welcome* by Winsome Pinnock. Linked to this theme is the demoralising effect of exodus and exile with its consequent crisis of identity and striving for self respect. Lennox Brown's *In the Autumn Room*, *Sweet Talk* by Michael Abensetts and *Nice* by Mustapha Matura are examples of these. The disintegration and separation of the family is seen in *Running Dream* by Trish Cooke and *Strange Fruit* by Cas Phillips.

Another theme is spirituality and its meaning in the lives of Black people. *Ritual* by Edgar White, Trish Cooke's *Running Dream* and Zindika's *Leonora's Dance* are typical of this.

Yet another theme involves the confrontation of and challenge to overt and institutional racism. *Ragamuffin* by Amani Naptali is a prime example of this, together with Farrukh Dhondy's *Mama Dragon* and *Trinity* by Edgar White.

Plays set in the Caribbean featuring social and political issues have been a natural part of the work of those British based writers born in the Caribbean. These plays suggest a longing for home, which can also be seen in *Zerri's Choice* by Sandra Yarr. Black British plays are constantly changing and maturing to meet changes in the social and political life of Britain, as Black people put down deeper roots in British society.

We can expect that play writing will gain in confidence and will continue to draw on a wide range of cultural influences such as music, rap, dance, street culture and new ones which will no doubt emerge and thereby broaden the form and content of the plays that will supply a pool of future texts and productions.

Performing Arts International
1996, Vol. 1, Part 2, pp. 57–63
Reprints available directly from the publisher
Photocopying permitted by license only

Panel: Present Practice
Notes on Becoming an Artist

Michael McMillan

Writer and Director. He is a published playwright and has been Artistic Director of Double Edge Theatre Company. He has both T.I.E. and lecturing experience. He approaches collaborative and devised work holistically, drawing integratedly from dance, visual arts or music, in combination with text.

At school, they told us that Shakespeare was the greatest playwright who ever wrote in the English language and if you didn't understand him and appreciate him, then the problem wasn't Shakespeare, the problem was you, and you were therefore stupid. Well I was stupid, because I couldn't understand what he was on about most of the time, much less relate to his world.

When I was fifteen, I wrote an essay entitled *Power to the Black Youth* for a competition in the *West Indian World*. To my shock, I won a three week trip to FESTAC '77 (The 2nd World Festival of Black Arts and Culture) in Nigeria. Were they jealous at school! Three weeks off school, all expenses paid, travelling outside England for the first time and on a plane as well. I was going to somewhere I had only read about and which I'd begun to realise was important to my roots: Africa.

The experiences, the smells, images, colours, people, left an imprint on me which I carry still today and most significantly for this talk, I worked back stage on Micheal Abbensetts' play *Sweet Talk* which was performed at the newly built National Theatre in Lagos. While I don't remember much of the play, I do remember the excitement of being around black people who were creating art. Unconsciously it was a world I wanted to be part of, if only as a means of completing my rite of passage in finding my identity as a young black person growing up in Britain.

It was not until we read Shelagh Delaney's play *A Taste of Honey* at school, that I was inspired to write my first play, and to write about my own experience. After FESTAC '77, anything was possible, I had the juice. For me *A Taste of Honey* had real characters, who spoke a real language, about real situations, real conflicts, real problems. I felt that I could relate to it. *The School Leaver* simply fell out from this cathartic process – not much on technique, but big on raw honesty.

Writing is a craft. It takes a long time to nurture, develop and perfect and I still have a lot to learn. Like many practitioners, my training has been through experience. The point here is that black arts practice has seen a renaissance in spite of the fact that while a token more black people are getting access to training today, the pedagogical framework, ideology, curricula and ethos are still very much eurocentric. The drama schools and performing and related arts education system is out of step with a multi-cultural, much less cross-cultural, theatre and performance world which has emerged over the past three decades.

Since the 19th Century, black performers have graced the English stage, from the seminal influence of Ira Aldridge and his contemporaries such as Morgan Smith, through to Paul Robeson's monumental impact on Shakespearean theatre during the 1930s and 1940s. If we are to talk of black theatre as a movement, as a body of work written by, produced, directed, and performed by black people, CLR James's play, *The Black Jacobins*, produced in the 1930s, signifies that beginning.

To talk of black theatre, is to talk of a Black Arts movement and like similar movements in cultural history, it has emerged to broaden our understanding of the world, to sensitise us emotionally and intellectually, and bring blackness to our consciousness, to challenge the status quo. And, like all movements, it will cease once it has achieved its goal. Consequently, black theatre is a cultural political movement, it does not describe an aesthetic – yet it implies one.

…when you write a play about Black people, white people can assume that this is a finite model of the Black community and that is what the Black community is about. There is a whole range of material available about the white community from *Confessions of a Window Cleaner* to *Apocalypse Now* and it is clear that white society is complex and full of contradictions… White people can afford the luxury of looking at themselves in three dimensions and Black people in two dimensions…

(Caryl Phillips – Artrage: Nov 1982)

Black theatre does not wholly describe my practice, as the term black is a political reference, embracing African-Caribbean and Asian. I am an African-Caribbean Black British person of colour, whose ancestors were African, Indian, Portuguese and Scottish, whose parents were farmers from St. Vincent, who grew up in a working class home, who was born in England and educated in an English education system, who went to a bourgeois institution for higher education, who is an able-bodied, heterosexual male… I think I'll stop there, because the list can go on. The point is that the notion of some 'essentialist' black experience out there waiting to be captured is a myth.

I have been inspired in a local and diasporic sense by Lorraine Hansberry's *A Raisin in the Sun* and the works of Edgar White, such as

The Nine Night, George C. Wolfe's *The Colored Museum,* and *Amain Napthali's Ragamuffin,* among many others. Yet Augusto Boal's *Theatre of the Oppressed* forms part of my eclectic appropriation as well as the critical theories of Brecht, Eisenstein, and a range of performance or live art, visual arts, film and TV.

As Guillermo Gomez-Pena argues, the job of the artist is to force open the matrix of reality to admit unsuspected possibilities. As a writer and theatre practitioner in performance and mixed media, language is the tweezers or crowbar I use to open up these worlds; language – its meaning, its subversion and its transformation, whether oral, textual, visual, physical, spiritual, meta-physical – is the means by which I communicate. Theatre is experience, it is 'edutainment' not entertainment.

'I don't think that you can affect people unless you touch them or upset them. I want to change people's perceptions and not write something they can forget easily and one of the ways you can do this is to make people angry and outraged, but the content has to be honest.'

(Caryl Phillips – Artrage: Nov 1982)

On Duty by Michael McMillan. Produced as a stage play in 1983 and subsequently as a drama/documentary video for Channel 4's Eleventh Hour Series (from which this still is 0taken), broadcast April 1984. The text is published by Akira Press. Photograph by Lance Watson.

For example, when I wrote *On Duty,* I was not only exploring the story of a black woman health worker becoming politicised after twenty years of working in, and sustaining the NHS, I was writing about my parent's generation who arrived in 'the mother country' to find a hostile reception, yet struggled on in spite of that.

A number of my early plays were in a naturalistic, social-realist, so-called 'community theatre', tradition. I became frustrated with this convention as it did not enable me to explore the more complex, often invisible, essences of life. As Brecht argues, art is not revolutionary unless it is revolutionary in form. I became interested in non-naturalistic aesthetics.

I began to realise that as a practitioner, I inherited a history of ancient African cultural and artistic traditions which could be juxtaposed with contemporary perspectives. Ancient African ritual arts are a holistic fusion of drama, dance, movement, song, music, poetry and visual arts. As a writer I was part of an oral tradition with a long legacy going back to the African griot and that tradition is very much evident today in black popular culture, in performance poetry, rap, ragga, calypso.

'You know in African tradition the magic happens in the journey *to* the drum. It's not the music that comes from the drum, the drum actually takes you into it.'
(Keith Antar Mason – The Hittite Empire)

This phenomenon is not new, it is simply the expression of mind, body and spirit, that esoteric feeling you get when you hear the blues of Billie Holliday, the jazz of Miles Davis, the gospel singing at church, when you dance to James Brown, when you play mass at carnival.

It is the fusion of contemporary perspective, that is for me the avant garde:

"The avant garde is no longer in the front but in the margins". To be avant garde... is to contribute to the decentralisation of art. To be avant garde means to be able to cross the border back and front between art and politically significant territory, be it inter-racial, immigration, ecology, homelessness, AIDS or violence towards disenfranchised communities and Third World countries. "To be avant garde means to perform and exhibit in both artistic and non-artistic contexts: to operate in the world, not just the art world."
(Guillermo Gomez-Pena)

Critical debates in film theory and visual arts formed a catalyst in my process of becoming. I was introduced to performance art, and I collaborated with the black mixed-media artist Keith Piper in creating *Portrait of a Shopping Centre as a Cathedral*, a performance installation. Performed in Dalston Cross Shopping Centre, Hackney (Art & Society, October 1990), it was a parody on the cultural appropriation of black popular culture in the commodification of lifestyle and of how the Shopping Centre/Mall had become a holy relic in which we were enslaved to labels and the big hype. Setting the piece site-specifically

Portrait of a Shopping Centre as a Cathedral, a collaborative performance installation by Michael McMillan and Keith Piper, performed in Dalston Cross Shopping Centre, October 1990. Photograph by Ingrid Polland.

addressed issues of marginal invisibility, control and appropriation, where a new high-tech shopping centre, devoid of black businesses, had been erected next door to North London's most vibrant black market, Ridley Road. The environment made the work, as much as the interaction with shoppers and passersby. I was also interested in utilising the practice of call and response, a tradition emerging out of the black religious movements and theatre.

In fact, the piece was constructed so that spectator/audience participation became intrinsic to its meaning. I found a freedom of expression in the spoken word/poetry and drama, challenging the body, mind, voice and soul, in time and space. This process of fusing performance/live action and text, offered opportunities to experiment with form, style, genre and presentation and complemented the fragmented and chaotic nature of cultural identities and difference, and the desire to break out of convention and operate on the edge.

Double Edge embraces this thirst for innovation, *Raggamuffin* was fresh because it not only articulated, for the first time, the sentiments of a whole generation of black youth, but used very simply black popular cultural forms which the audience could directly relate to. Using a sound system, and the lyrics of the dance hall and ragga, enabled the audience to participate, to get involved. *Raggamuffin* essentially broke the fourth wall, as a divide between the audience and the stage and performers. In coming to see *Raggamuffin*, the audience were coming to church, they became transformed into a congregation. This process is in the tradition of Caribbean popular theatre, much less African arts and culture. And while many may dismiss the Bups phenomenon as sexist and crude, it has brought a Caribbean popular form of theatre to Britain, as well as working African-Caribbean audiences, who are not alienated but allowed to comment, 'cuss', participate and own.

Working with Double Edge, where the stimuli come from the ancient African ritual arts, with contemporary perspectives, has enabled the creation of new languages of communication and interaction. Consequently, my most recent play *Invisible* became a multi-media performance piece inspired by Ralph Ellison's novel *Invisible Man* and the writing of Franz Fanon. It was a meditation on the psycho-sexual experience of the black male over five hundred year. It was challenging, deliberately so, and for some it was uncomfortable, yet I felt that

'We must have the courage to turn our gaze inward and begin to raise the touchy issues that most of us avoided in the past decade: Men of colour are active participants in the history of sexism and (European) women share the blame in the history of racism. we must accept this with valour and dignity.'

(Guillermo Gomez-Pena)

Ritual refers to a more esoteric, spiritual practice. The process of finding the creative voice is focused on the spoken word coming from within the artist's inner-self. Exploration is improvisational, the artist is taken on a journey with words, sounds and power of voice-sounds/chants, drums/ instruments and the movement of the body. It is like the improvisational process of jazz; I term this 'the jazz aesthetic', just as improvisation is a part of African-Caribbean culture.

Jazzoetry

Rhythms and Sounds
In leaps and Bounds
Scales and notes and endless quotes
Hey! Black soul being told

Hypnotising while improvising is mentally
Appetising off on a tangent
Ain't got a cent
Searching, soaring, exploring,

Seek and you shall find
More time, more time
More time, more time
More time, more time...
(The Last Poets)

Performing Arts International
1996, Vol. 1, Part 2, pp. 65–75
Reprints available directly from the publisher
Photocopying permitted by license only

© 1996 OPA (Overseas Publishers Association)
Amsterdam B.V. Published in The Netherlands
by Harwood Academic Publishers
Printed in India

Panel: Young Practitioners

Maureen Hibbert, Stuart Taylor, Patricia Elcock and Ninder Billing

Maureen Hibbert, Stuart Taylor, Patricia Elcock and Ninder Billing are four young graduates who have relatively recently come through higher education, Maureen and Stuart as mature students, and have made careers for themselves in the arts and the media. They were invited to speak at the conference about their experience of higher education and to what extent their studies or training contributed to their personal development as well as preparing them for their present work and future ambitions. The idea for this panel arose from talking with graduates who had studied Black Theatre at Middlesex and who identified specific ways in which that study had provided them with opportunities and perspectives not gained elsewhere.

The following papers are mainly edited transcripts of presentations, although Stuart Taylor's paper is predominantly taken from the written version he submitted. They offer four very distinctive voices. Differently, but equally strongly, each demands our attention and our respect.

MAUREEN HIBBERT: Actress. Her acting work ranges from playing the Prosecutor in the powerful and ground-breaking theatre production *Ragamuffin*, by Double Edge Theatre Company, to playing actress Tracy in the dramatisation of Hanif Kureishi's *Buddha of Suburbia* for BBC TV.

After accepting the invitation from Ruth to contribute to this conference, I read the brief very carefully to make sure I understood it. I perceived the question to be: 'What, or where, is the link between academia and the rest of the world?' So that's my covering umbrella, and I'm just going to tell you about myself really.

I was educated during the grammar school era, with its echoes of the eleven plus, and I failed the test, so I entered the alternative secondary modern system. I moved to further education with six 'O' levels and a year later entered nurse training with eight. I qualified as a State Registered Nurse and worked in a Coronary Care Unit which involves looking after patients who have had heart attacks or heart dysfunctional problems. I worked there for a year and then came to London to study psychiatric nursing.

The skills that I felt I subsequently brought with me when I came to study for a degree at Middlesex Polytechnic, ranged from having the ability to make important decisions in a highly pressured environment through to experience in expressing myself, both personally and professionally, in highly interactive and dynamic situations. As a student of pre-Black Theatre Studies, my connection then to Black Theatre work was via a Proposition Module at the begining of my second year and an Independent Module in my third. Both of these took place outside the Polytechnic but were assessed internally:

If yu invite me inna yu yard, yu mus have something inna yu pot fe mi fe nam.

I often felt that as a student accepted into the institution on the merits of my academic qualifications and cultural perspective, that the academic side of performance was supported but that the cultural side was largely ignored. The theoretical collating and evaluating made me think in a formalised way, observing and accepting or not accepting the rules laid down and then at times testing the parameters: eurocentric versus global. At present I still find myself testing them: the subtle misunderstandings and the overt racism. Nowadays, I become involved in a project because of, and to celebrate with others, the differences on the one hand or the shared beliefs on the other, or I don't get involved at all. If I go into something and I realise that it is not going to celebrate individuals' sharing, then I talk about it, in the hope that both sides can find a common language and understanding. Sometimes, though, you have to eat! I'm fortunate enough to have an agent who has an understanding of my personal and cultural perspectives, whilst offering to guide my career with concern for commercial considerations. Even so, I may not always accept his offers. *Ragamuffin*, *The Real McCoy* and *JamaicanAirman* were celebrations of beliefs I shared. *Pan Project*, which I worked on in England and in India, *Stamping, Shouting and Singing Home* and *Buddha of Suburbia*, celebrated difference in their perspectives.

I feel that had this wider range of cultural expression been part of the curriculum I studied and been accepted as valid, studying Shakespeare alongside The Mahabharata or Beckett with Walcott, there would have been less marginalisation. I believe that the combination of my training together with my own cultural perspective, taught me to find a way to express myself with integrity. In that, it has been successful. But there remains a lack of respect in mainstream education for new and different inputs. All successful instituitions have a common denominator: they take on board new ideas, or old ones with 'today' written on them; fortunately for all of us concerned, individuality will always find a way.

In finding the time and space to think about these points raised by the conference, and in writing them down, Miles Davis was my inspiration.

STUART TAYLOR: Performance Artist, Educationalist and Researcher. His creative work is interdisciplinary and cross-media. At the time of publication of these conference papers he has taken up the post of Gallery Director at f. stop Media Station, Bath.

New Soul Geographies

In order to make some sense of where I am today as an artist and as a man, a black man, I thought it pertinent to offer some brief biographical details. This to me seems the most direct way of illuminating the journey I have thus far travelled during the past twenty years and I hope gives a sense of the paths I have yet to tread.

My formative years were spent in Torquay, a medium-sized seaside resort in Devon. My mother heralds from Birmingham, my father-biological from St. Kitts and my father-legal from Torquay. Being born and raised in the early sixties in the west country was, on reflection, an unusual experience, on several counts.

Firstly, my mother is a white woman, then ostracised by her family for having a relationship with a black man. My father-biological was, and remains, unaware of my coming into the world; my father-legal was, and is, a man of very private and passive character who I believe has demonstrated great moral strength in the face of quite considerable prejudice. I say this without intending to diminish the strength, resilience and care my mother has exhibited – at, I think, some considerable cost to herself – over the years. Further, I had in later years two sisters, the fruit of my mother's and father-legal's relationship. I wish to stress they have been as close to, and supportive of, me as I could wish and we continue to share a warm and emotionally rich relationship.

As you might begin to see, this is not exactly an everyday story. The context in which I grew up is I think atypical of the black experience here in Britain and perhaps Asia, the Caribbean and America. I state this in so much as for the first eighteen years of my life the cultural environment I grew up in was effectively white. In a town of around 250,000 people I was one of perhaps ten 'non-Europeans'. There was I think one other black male at the secondary school I attended. Until I spent time at art school I don't recall seeing any Asian or Arab people, even then a tiny, tiny minority.

As a consequence of this experience I had no significant concept of black culture or models of black men and women and their respective achievements to aspire towards. My concept of blackness was frankly of difference, otherness and being the odd-one-out and too often the exotic freak or scapegoat. My sense of blackness was through the ignorant eyes of a white person.

In recounting this history it's difficult to be very specific about feelings and ideas I held concerning my status in relation to family and peers, other than to say I exuded a natural confidence with a broad streak of aggression and wildness. The wildness was a kind of confused torment about just how I came to be who I was, where I was. Over the years I've begun to explore this experience with more and more clarity and informed purpose. So without wishing to dwell overmuch on my domestic background I feel it appropriate to move on to my educational develoment as this perhaps pertains more tangibly to the conference topic.

I displayed a rebellious intelligence at secondary school and was an aggressive individual. This was a result of the situation I found myself in regarding my family and community. The aggression was I suppose partly a defence mechanism and partly a channel for the confusion I felt for the first fifteen years or so of my life. I spent most of my time in school enjoying teasing and disrupting my teachers and being regarded as something of a rogue by my peers. Although I did not apply myself particularly I did obtain sufficient qualifications to gain a place on a graphic design course at the local art school. This was a deliberate move on my part as I had tagged along on a visit to the art school and decided it was my next destination. I had received no career-counselling during my school years. I saw the art school as a ticket out of Torquay and the small-mindedness I had become aware of with its limitations for personal fulfilment in a social and professional context. Also, the subjects I had enjoyed and engaged with the most during my school career, beyond athletics, were English, History, Drama and Drawing.

I felt for the first time in my life, apart from the empathy I experienced with the Punk/Dada movement – having passed through terrace hooliganism – that the world of art was a place where I might begin to grow and discover and express myself.

I applied myself with quite a rigorous consistency during my three years studying graphic design and gained a broad foundation experience to a range of media and art techniques alongside art history, sociology and applied design skills. Upon graduating from the course I moved to London, which was I suppose a significant step in my development. I chose to move to Brixton as I knew it was a place where black people lived alongside Bohemian whites. At that time in the early eighties Brixton was a relaxed and exciting village-like quarter, through my eyes anyway. It was, nonetheless, a huge shock to my system being amongst so many black people, and for the second time in my life I was in a state of confusion and bewilderment. This process was taking place at the same time as my searching for employment as a dreadlocked designer in a very white and conservative design profession.

Suffice it to say that I did not have a great deal of success in finding employment. I did, though, obtain two positions. One of them with an international advertising agency in Mayfair. I think there was some genuine interest in my talent, however the position lasted only a few weeks. I found myself in a very fragile state of mind, trying to reconcile my experience in Torquay with living in Brixton, adjusting to the city and working in an exclusively white environment. I was working on campaigns for pet food etc. which to my radicalised but inarticulate mind were facile. After leaving the position I moved on to the other end of the spectrum and the other side of town. I worked, again for a short time, with a national Asian youth organisation. The offices were based in Southall and for the first time I felt that I fitted somewhere without the need for curtailment, explanation or performing. I was able to talk and articulate aspects of my experience with work colleagues and be taken seriously. I found out about political exiles resident in Britain, about some of the socio-political history of modern India and the British-Asian experience.

Unfortunately, due to the demands of the job, the fragility of my mind at that time and my lack of experience, this post lasted only a few months. After which time I drifted for a while without gaining further employment as a graphic designer. I was feeling trapped by the lack of vision, creatively speaking, on the part of clients and employers. I actually sought no further employment in the field. I moved around the fringes of the experimental music scene and the drug scene. I began serious practice of yoga and going to see film at independent cinemas alongside taking in much visual art.

Without going into great detail, as a consequence of my involvement with the drug scene I ended up in Germany spending one year in prison. In many respects this was, at the age of twenty, a lucky break. I was in a position where I was able to take stock of my life and some of the factors which had shaped it.

Over the year I religiously practised yoga, learned German, read a great deal of literature, played a lot of chess and lived a life of stern self-discipline. One thought returns to you every day when you are living in a single cell in a prison on foreign soil: what are you going to do with your life after this? In the beginning I didn't know. Then after some months I had a lengthy list of likely and implausible pursuits. After a year of constant attention, on returning to England I had five possible directions, all requiring further study: psychology, philosophy, anthropology, performance or literature.

The first thing I did on returning to my home town was to find the first available classes in dance. Second, I enrolled at the local college for a double A-level course in psychology and English literature/language compressed into one year. The academic study of psychology and literature gave me a formal and critical framework in which to locate the insights I had gained prior to, and during, my internment, as well as helping kick start my intellectual muscles. The dance classes snowballed from once-a-week jazz dance sessions to ballet and contemporary technique. I was travelling up to one hundred miles a week to attend rehearsals, workshops, courses and classes in dance and movement-theatre skills.

Very quickly the notion of an academic route for my life lost credence and I decided that performance would be the vehicle for my ongoing intellectual artistic and professional development. I arrived at the position where I considered the previously mentioned interests in anthropology, literature, psychology, philosophy could all be somehow integrated within the field of performance. I continued to devote more and more time to gaining performance skills. I was able to support myself with a range of small-time jobs, such as Tarzan-o-gram, barman and plasterer's mate until I obtained a good position as a language tutor for several seasons. Being something of a passionate user and believer in literature and language and a performer as well, the role of teacher suited me well. In fact education has been a mainstay of my professional work as an artist since 1989.

The result of my newly-won determination and focus was to gain a place at the Laban Centre from which I graduated in 1989. I studied on the Dance Theatre Certificate course. I had the opportunity to study at other centres at degree level but chose a non-degree route at Laban as I was confident of my intellectual and artistic aspirations but wanted a rigorous and disciplined technical training. This I got in no uncertain terms. In short I had a contentious and rebellious time at Laban. It was a very passionate three years, during which I represented my year group for two consecutive years, was an organiser in the student union and initiated a widely publicised student choreography platform and graduation show. I think I knew from the outset that ultimately I wanted to produce my own works upon graduation. Choreography and directing were certainly the areas that inspired me and most satisfied me artistically and intellectually.

Upon graduating from Laban I assembled a group of colleagues with my partner Jane Buchanan and between us we produced a company-devised work which we presented for one week at the Fringe Festival in Edinburgh. This was my first taste of making art for real. It was very, very, very intense and passionate, a real trial by fire. Having survived this first adventure as an independent artist I sought further opportunities to be involved in works by other people or to initiate my own work. I was, and remain, most interested and motivated to initiate my own projects. Since

1989 I have initiated, directed or choreographed and performed in seven performance works of growing ambition and complexity:

H2O – A piece exploring the role(s) and misuses of water in society.
The Comfort of Strangers 1 – A piece exploring notions of private and public disclosures and voyeurism.
The Comfort of Strangers 2 – The proscenium version of the work transposed to a site-specific location imcorporating a light installation and projection.
Interspace – A work exploring the relationship between site, film and live presences.
Games of Choice and Chance – A site-specific work illustrating the psycho-emotional manoeuvring within adult relationships.
Promiscuous Tangle – A piece exploring the use of text and movement with an actress; again delving into the make up and passion expressed and suppressed within relationships.

All of these works took place between 1989 and 1992. Original music was commissioned for each project. Some of the works received project funding from public agencies.

A further significant juncture in my development occurred in 1992 when I received two scholarships from the Harold Ham Wingate Foundation and the British American Arts Association. These enabled me to begin an ongoing research programme into interactive digital media, performance practice an interculturalism. I explored these three fields of activity in North America and the Caribbean, travelling to San Francisco, Los Angeles, Atlanta, Chicago, Philadelphia, New York and St. Kitts. My rationale for undertaking the trip was threefold. Firstly, I needed to get out of the work cycle I had developed as I had reached a point of exhaustion from making works back to back. Secondly, I wanted to engage in these three specific areas outside of my common frame of reference in order to situate myself in a broader cultural and historical context. Lastly I needed fresh stimulus and to rediscover my motivations and needs for making art.

In the time that has flowed since the end of 1992 I have been involved in speaking at a conference and contributing to cultural publications. I have also featured in an award winning video-work directed by Alison Murray. My most recent new work is a piece called *Forensic Fictions 'New Soul Geographies'*, presented at the ICA in the Autumn as part of a season of work by black artists exploring cultural identity. This was my first piece in which I have made explicit my understanding of being a black man and the factors that impact on my life, historical and contemporary. It was a complex piece of work, utilising diverse media including photography, video, ice sculptures, movement, action drawing, text, large format projection, rice and candles alongside original music and live mixing.

My concerns as an artist, moving now into the middle phase of my life, are to continue exploring the role(s) and impact of technology on our lives, the possibility of deep communication through aesthetics and live performance and the emancipatory potential in artistic and educational practice. My work is informed by my readings of history and critical theory alongside my experience as a father/a black man/cultural nomad/internationalist/shape shifter and member of the global Diaspora.

These are the stories, these are the truths, we need to engender a re-orientation of discourse on cultural identity. If you don't ask questions then beware of lies. Who is writing your future?

PATRICIA ELCOCK: Writer and Performer. Patricia has been commissioned by Carlton to contribute as a writer to the popular TV series *Desmonds.*

My name's Patricia Elcock and I'm 23 years old and this is my first year outside education. I'm writing at the moment, and I'm more amazed than anyone by this. I can't even call myself a writer yet, so when I am given this little badge to wear saying 'Writing for Carlton TV' I ask, Who? Me?

You know it happened quite by accident and there have been a lot of lucky breaks. I was in this programme on TV and some people saw me and invited me to write a script, – yes, it's all fairy tale stuff.

When I was invited to contribute here today, I started to think about Black Theatre Studies at college, which I'd not really thought about before. At the time, you think about it in terms of the three thousand word essay and the practical assessment with a back up, and that's all, but now I'm thinking more about how it relates to me as a person, to me as a creator, as a writer and performer. I operate on two levels. Level one is the skill and the talent. However little or much talent there is, you need the skill to dig in and pull the talent out. And then you need the attitude, this is the second level. You need the attitude to put that skill or that talent into practice. Black theatre for me at college, was like a rediscovery, it was an awakening. Up until that point I'd been quite content to sit through classes and let the lecturers argue between themselves about Ibsen or about Brecht's didacticism. Black Theatre Studies was *the* class for debate. Discussions would spill over from class into the canteen afterwards and then we'd be calling each other up later to carry on over the phone, because we were just set on fire by this thing. Here was a subject that was relevant to me. It was to register with me and my life in a way no other class had done. For a lot of the time at college a lot of what you do doesn't matter to you, you have to admit it, you just get through it. But Black Theatre mattered.

So in the first Black Theatre module I did, it was coming round to assessment time and I couldn't think what to do and then suddenly I got the idea for this character. Some friends and I were talking and this character came to me. I wrote a monologue for myself and this is how all this writing began. I have to give credit back to this class, credit where it is due. This character was in my head and I could hear the voice and it was really real to me and so I wrote the monologue and performed it and it proved to me that I could write for the ear again. I always liked writing as a child, dazzling the family with my stories: 'Mum listen to this!' But then you go to school and there's no fun in writing, it's technical, it's clinical, it's all about grammar and you feel you're strangled. By the time I hit 'A' levels, writing had become a cynical exercise. When I started writing for the ear again, I could enjoy it, and I could see that it was a way of expressing myself and of making that voice come across directly. The monologue is all about intimacy and immediacy.

One of the themes I picked up in Black Theatre Studies was black theatre as documentation of black experience. Although first and foremost an entertainment, the monologue I wrote was a document of a particular experience as I saw it.

Another of the things that strikes me about black theatre, and something I try to hold on to, is the way it empowers. Black Theatre takes action, makes things happen, gives a voice to unheard people, ideas and sentiments. It's up to the writer to make the voice heard. Black Theatre, as a study, validated much of what I thought and felt instinctively. It made a space on an often oppressive syllabus for a person's creative self-expression. In that space I grew in confidence, and confidence is the greatest eye opener, allowing you to see everything as possible. So when somebody offered me a place on a sitcom writers' course, I was brazen enough to accept it, having done nothing of the sort before, and I'm learning on the job.

There is a lot of negative criticism about the state of black theatre and the plight of the black artist/performer. People complain that musicals are the only black productions to make it to the West End. While this may be a valid point, it isn't an argument I want to get into. My energies are better spent in creating work which will stand as its own testimony, rather than berating what has gone before. You have to say: I have my voice and it's going to be heard. It's all about the attitude of people like the Bibi Crew or The Posse. Whatever you think about that style of entertainment, you have to look at the fact that these are two groups of individuals who have said, 'I'm gonna do something', and they've done it.

Black theatre has long since earned its place on drama syllabi, both as an area in its own right and within other areas of study such as Contemporary Theatre, Physical Theatre and so on. It makes you question, it makes you look at what you can do and it gives you confidence to use what is within you.

That is all I have to say.

NINDER BILLING: Researcher and Assistant Television Producer. Her recent work has included researching for the series *Black Bag* for BBC TV.

Over the last couple of weeks, I've been filming with a lot of young successful Asian professionals, all of whom have invariably turned round to me and said, 'How long did it take you to be an Assistant Producer? How did you think this is what I want to do?' So I've had to think 'Where did I get that from?' My education was very white. When I got to Middlesex, I was the only Asian on my course, and then Black Theatre came along. I think it was the first year Black Theatre was offered, so I didn't know what to expect. Looking back on it, it did give me what all three of the people here have spoken about, that sense of validity, discovering that opportunity to articulate my own experience. The one thing I didn't like about Black Theatre was that there wasn't any Asian Theatre in it. It was black politically but it was actually Afro-Caribbean Black, so within the Black Theatre course I did my own independent study at Tara Arts. When I came across Asian Theatre I was absolutely stunned: all these Asian people being creative and talking about things that I was feeling. That was what was really important to me and what, in a roundabout way, got me my first job in journalism. I did a bit of radio and I did a bit of independent television and I ended up in the BBC in multicultural programmes. It's a bit like Black Theatre in a way, multicultural programming, a kind of ghettoisation or marginalisation, but I liked it so much I've stayed there. It's good for me and it gives me the opportunity to make programmes that I think need to be made.

I feel there is undeniably a different experience for Asian people in this country to the Afro-Caribbean person. When I look around I see Afro-Caribbean people much more confident about where they are in this country, and I see my Asian peer group only just beginning to emerge with that sense of validity and that sense of confidence. That just-emerging confidence is being reflected in the new art movement as well. If you look around at British Asians, whatever that term means, you feel the need to be there. I don't know if I'm at the cutting edge or am actually being a part of it, but being in my position means I can document development and possibly and give it publicity and make other people aware of it.

Everything that comes out of multicultural programming comes in for flack; the black press and other interested black parties, will always say we've failed in some way, will always say we've been exploitative, or that we've talked about the things that shouldn't be talked about, that we should give positive images. That's a big dilemma. To have that debate and to come to some kind of conclusion, then you have to have a sense of yourself and a sense of what you want to do and that is what I relate back to my study of black theatre. I can sit down and talk to people about why I make programmes about black on black gun violence. I'll readily talk about why I made programmes about prostitution in the Asian community. I feel that it is necessary for us to talk about these things because if we don't talk about them then other people will do so without knowing what they're talking about. That really is my feeling. I know other people disagree with this. What comes out of that is more positive I think than just making programmes about the achievements of black people, because the achievers are there. We have to achieve ourselves, as well as just documenting what other people have achieved.

Being where I am has been very strange. I just tread my path within the BBC and every now and then I'll get called to comment on something. Recently I took part in the regular Radio 4 arts programme *Kaleidoscope*. It stunned me that *Kaleidoscope* wanted to look at Asian arts. There is a whole new development in the media and performing arts, like Yuva the dance group, the film *Bhaji on the Beach*, the theatre production *Moti Roti, Puttli Chunni*. People are actually coming forward and claiming, 'We can do this. We're Asian, and we can use our experience'. A lot of the time I have felt that Asians have been observing the African-Caribbean experience, and, yes, I can emphathise with that, but now this new confidence, this new found sense of self is coming forward, which for me was something to do with Black Theatre Studies, and it gives me great joy. We can only go from strength to strength in this.

My department has recently decided that we're going to develop some black drama, some Asian drama, Asian sit-com, and I'm thinking that I'm actually in a unique position as I look around at the people I'm working with. None of them has studied black theatre, so while everyone's interested, none of them has got that informed interest. You suddenly find yourself in that position and you feel grateful; I feel very privileged to have studied black theatre because now I can give back and I think that's probably the most important thing to come out of it. If we can find ourselves in positions where we can give back, and we want to do so, then what more can you ask from an academic background than to make it a reality.

My future hopes are to carry on doing more of the same, and doubtless I'll incur more wrath from black people, but I suppose we just have to stick that out.

Performing Arts International
1996, Vol. 1, Part 2, pp. 77–82
Reprints available directly from the publisher
Photocopying permitted by license only

© 1996 OPA (Overseas Publishers Association)
Amsterdam B.V. Published in The Netherlands
by Harwood Academic Publishers
Printed in India

Black Theatre
Selected Bibliography

The following Selected Bibliography concentrates on Black and Asian British Theatre, together with Caribbean Theatre, which often crosses over between Britain and the Caribbean, addressing themes and issues of shared concern or heritage. Also included, here, are shorter sections on African-American and African Theatres, with particular attention given to selecting plays that have been produced in Britain in the last fifteen years.

Occasionally a playscript has been included by a white playwright, because of its significance in black theatre development, and in those instances the playwright's name is marked with an asterisk. Otherwise, playscripts listed are by black playwrights. No distinction has been made between black and white writers of secondary material listed here.

Joan-Ann Maynard's contribution to the compilation of the playscripts lists is gratefully acknowledged.

A. Ruth Tompsett

1 Playscripts
Black and Asian British and Caribbean

Ahmad, R. *Song for Sanctuary* in: George, K. (ed.) *Six plays by Black and Asian Women*, London: Aurora Metro Press 1993

Ali, T. & Brenton, H. *Iranian Nights* London: Nick Hern 1989

Bains, S.H. *Blood* London: Methuen 1989

Baku, S. *3 Plays of Our Time* Trinidad and Tobago 1984

Carriere, J. *The Mahabharata* London: Methuen 1988

Celeste, M. *Obeah* in: Keeffe, B. (ed.) *The 1988 Award-Winning New Plays Verity Bargate* London: Methuen 1989

Chowdhry, M. *Monsoon* in: George, K. (ed.) *Six Plays by Black and Asian Women Writers*, London: Aurora Metro Press 1993

Cooke, T. *Back Street Mammy* in: Harwood, K. (sel.) in *First Run 2* London: Nick Hern 1990

Cooke, T. *Running Dream,* in: George, K. (ed.) *Six plays by Black and Asian Women Writers*, London: Aurora Metro Press 1993

Cooper, M. *Heartgame* in *Plays by Women: Eight* London: Methuen 1990

Dhondy, F. *Romance, Romance* and *The Bride* London: Faber and Faber 1985

Dodgson, E. *Motherland* 'West Indian Women to Britain in the 1950s' Oxford and London: Heinemann Educational 1980

Ellis, M. *Chameleon* in: Brewster, Y. (ed.) *Black Plays* London: Methuen 1987

John, E. *Moon on a Rainbow Shawl* London: Faber & Faber 1958

Kureishi, H. *My Beautiful Launderette* London: Faber and Faber 1986

Kureishi, H. *Borderline* London: Methuen/Royal Court 1981

Kureishi, H. *Outskirts and Other Plays* London: Faber and Faber 1992

Lovelace, E. *The Dragon Can't Dance* in: Brewster, Y. (ed.) *Black Plays: Two* London: Methuen 1989

McMillan, M. *On Duty* London: Akira Press 1986

Matura, M. *Collected Plays* London: Methuen 1992

Ogidi, A. *Ragamuffin* in: Mortimer, J. (ed.) *Young Playwrights' Festival*, BBC Radio Drama, London: BBC 1988

Oshodi, M. *Blood Sweat and Fears* in: Brewster, Y. (ed.) *Black Plays: Two* London: Methuen 1989

Phillips, C. *Playing Away* London: Faber and Faber 1987

Phillips, C. *Where There is Darkness* Oxford: Amber Lane Press 1982

Pinnock, W. *A Rock in Water* in: Brewster, Y. (ed.) *Black Plays: Two* London: Methuen 1989

Pinnock, W. *Leave Taking* in: Harwood, K. (sel.) *First Run* London: Nick Hern 1989

Pinnock, W. *A Hero's Welcome* in George, K. (ed.) *Six Plays by Black and Asian Women Writers*, London: Aurora Metro Press 1993

Raif, A. *Caving In* in *Plays by Women: Eight* London: Methuen 1990

Rhone, T. *Old Story Time and other Plays* (including *Smile Orange*) Harlow: Longman 1981

Rudet, J. *Basin* in: Brewster, Y. (ed.) *Black Plays* London; Methuen 1987

Rudet, J. *Money To Live* in: Remnant, M. (sel.) *Plays by Women: Vol.5* London: Methuen 1986

Selvon, S. *Eldorado West One* Leeds: Peepal Tree Press 1988

Syal, M. *My Sister-Wife* in: George, K. (ed.) *Six Plays by Black and Asian Women Writers* London: Aurora Metro Press 1993

Walcott, D. *The Joker of Seville* and *O Babylon!* London: Jonathan Cape 1979

Walcott, D. *Three Plays* New York: Farrar Straus, Giroux 1986

White, E. *The Nine Night* and *Ritual By Water* London: Methuen 1984

White, E. *Redemption Song and Other Plays* London and New York: Marion Boyars 1985

Zephaniah, B. *Job Rocking* in: Brewster, Y. (ed.) *Black Plays: Two* London: Methuen 1989

Zephaniah, B. *Hurricane Dub* in: *Young Playwrights' Festival 1988* London: BBC 1988

Zindika *Leonora's Dance* in: George, K. (ed.) *Six Plays by Black and Asian Women Writers* London: Aurora Metro Press 1993

Play Collections

Brewster, Y. (ed.) *Black Plays* London: Methuen 1987

Brewster, Y. (ed.) *Black Plays: Two* London: Methuen 1989

Brewster, Y. (ed.) *Black Plays: 3* London: Methuen 1995

George, K. (ed.) *Six Plays by Black and Asian Women Writers* London: Aurora Metro Press 1993

Hill, E. *Plays for Today* Harlow: Longman 1983

African-American

Baldwin, J. *Blues for Mister Charlie* New York: Laurel 1964
Baldwin, J. *The Amen corner* New York: Laurel 1990
Hansbury, L. *Raisin in the Sun* London: Methuen 1986 Also in: Remnant, M. (ed.) *Plays by Women Vol 5* London: Methuen 1986
Hughes, L. & Hurston, N.H. *Mule Bone* New York: Harper Collins 1991
Hughes, L. *Mulatto* in: Smalley, W. (ed.) *Five Plays by Langston Hughes* Bloomington: Indiana University Press 1963
Jones, L. (Baraka, A.) *Dutchman* London: Faber and Faber 1965
Kennedy, A. *In One Act* Minneapolis: University of Minnesota Press 1988
Kennedy, A. *A Rat's Mass* in: Couch, W.Jr. (ed.) *New Black Playwrights* Baton Rouge: Louisiana State University 1970
*O'Neill, E. *Emperor Jones* London: Macmillan 1960
*Sackler, H. *The Great White Hope* London: Faber and Faber 1971
Shange, N. *for colored girls who have considered suicide/when the rainbow is enuf* London: Methuen 1978
Shange, N. *Plays: One* London: Methuen 1992
White, E. *Les Femmes Noires* in *Redemption Song and Other Plays* London and New York: Marion Boyars 1985
Wilson, A. *Fences* and *Ma Rainey's Black Bottom* London: Penguin 1986
Wilson, A. *The Piano Lesson* New York and London: Plume/Penguin 1990
Wolfe, G.C. *The Colored Museum* London: Methuen 1987
Wolfe, G.C. *Spunk* New York: Theatre Communications Group 1991

Play Collections

Branch, W.B. (ed. & intro.) *Crosswinds* 'An Anthology of Black Dramatists in the Diaspora' U.S.A.: Bloomington & Indianapolis 1993
(Note: This Anthology includes plays by African and Caribbean, as well as African-American, playwrights)
Couch, W.Jr. (ed.) *New Black Playwrights* Baton Rouge: Louisiana State University 1968
Hatch, J.V. (ed.) *45 Plays by Black Americans 1847–1974* U.S.A.: Free Press 1974
Hill, E. (ed.) *Black Heroes: 7 Plays* U.S.A.: Applause 1989
King, W. and Milner, R. (ed.) *Black Drama Anthology* New York: Meridian/Penguin 1971
King, W.Jr. *New Plays for Black Theatre* Chicago: Third World Press 1989
Perkins, K.A. (ed.) *Black Female Playwrights: An Anthology of Plays before 1950* Bloomington and Indianapolis: Indiana University Press 1989
Perkins, K.A. & Uno, R. (ed.) *Contemporary Plays by Women of Color: An Anthology* London: Routledge 1996
(Note: This Anthology includes plays by African-American playwrights)
Wilkerson, M.B. (Sel.) *9 Plays by Black Women* New York: Mentor/Penguin Books 1986

South African

*Fugard, A., Kani, J. and Ntshona, W. *Sizwe Banzi is Dead* Oxford 1974 Also in: Fugard, A. *Statements: Three Plays* Oxford: Oxford University Press 1974
*Fugard, A. *My Children My Africa* London: Faber and Faber 1990

Junction Avenue Theatre Company, Purkey, M. (intro.) *Sophiatown* Johannesberg: David Philip 1988

Kente, G. *Too Late* in: Kavanagh, R.M. *South African People's Plays* Heinemann South Africa 1992

Mtwa, P., Ngema, M. and *Simon, B. *Woza Albert* London: Methuen 1983

Maponya, M. *The Hungry Earth* South Africa: Polypton 1981

Mutwa, C.V. *uNosilimela* in: Kavanagh, R.M. *South African People's Plays* Heinemann South Africa 1992

Shezi, M. *Shanti* in: Kavanagh, R.M. *South African People's Plays* Heinemann South Africa 1992

Play Collections

Gray, S. (sel.) *South African Plays* London: Nick Hern 1992

Kavanagh, R.M. *South African People's Plays* Heinemann South Africa 1992

Ndlovu, D. *Woza Africa: an Anthology of South African Plays* New York 1986

West African

Bandele, B. *Marching for Fausa* Oxford: Amber Lane Press 1993

Rotimi, O. *The Gods Are Not to Blame* Oxford: Oxford University Press 1971

Sowande, B. *Flamingo and Other Plays* Harlow: Longman 1986

Soyinka, W. *Collected Plays 1* and *2* Oxford: Oxford University Press 1974

2 Secondary Material
Black and Asian British and Caribbean Theatres

Arts Council *Theatre Is For All* London: Arts Council 1986

Arts Council *A Creative Future 'Towards a National Arts and Media Strategy'* London: HMSO 1993

Bharucha, R. *Theatre and The World* London and New York: Routledge 1993

Brewster, Y. *Black Plays* (see Introduction) London: Methuen 1987

Brewster, Y. *Black Plays: Two* (see Introduction) London: Methuen 1989

Brewster, Y. *Black Plays: 3* (see Introduction) London: Methuen 1995

Brook, P. *The Shifting Point* London: Methuen 1988

Chambers, C. *The Story of Unity Theatre* London: Lawrence & Wishart 1989

Corsbie, K. *Theatre in the Caribbean* London: Hodder and Stoughton 1984

Cohen, A. *Masquerade Politics* Providence and Oxford: Berg 1993

Craig, S. *Dreams & Deconstructions* Oxford: Amber Lane Press 1980

Dabydeen, D. *Black Presence in English Literature* Manchester: Manchester University Press 1985

Daniels, T. & Gerson, J. (ed.) *The Colour Black: Black Images in British Television* London: BFI 1989

Fryer, P. *Staying Power* London: Pluto 1986

Goodman, L. *Contemporary Feminist Theatres* London: Routledge 1993

Hill, E. *The Jamaican Stage 1655–1900*: 'A Profile of a Colonial Theatre' U.S.A.: University of Massachusetts Press 1992

Hill, E. *Shakespeare in Sable*: 'A History of Black Shakespearean Actors' U.S.A.: University of Massachusetts Press 1984

Hill, E. *The Trinidad Carnival*: 'Mandate for a National Theatre' Austin: University of Texas 1972

Itzin, C. *Stages in the Revolution* London: Methuen 1980

James, W. and Harris, C. *Inside Babylon*: 'The Caribbean Diaspora in Britain' London: Verso 1993

Jonas, G. *Dancing*: 'The Power of Dance Around the World' London: BBC Books 1992

Khan, N. *The Arts Britain Ignores* London: C.R.E. 1976

King, B. *West Indian Drama* Oxford: Oxford University Press 1995

Nettleford, R. *Inward Stretch, Outward Reach*: 'A Voice from the Caribbean' London and Basingstoke: Macmillan 1993

Nunley, J. and Bettelheim, J. *Carribean Festival Arts* U.S.A.: University of Washington Press 1988

Omotoso, K. *The Theatrical Into Theatre* London: New Beacon Books 1982

Owusu, K. *The Struggle for Black Arts in Britain* London: Comedia 1986

Owusu, K. *Storms of the Heart* London: Camden Press 1988

Owusu, K. & Ross, J. *Behind the Masquerade* London: Arts Media 1988

Phillips, C. *The European Tribe* London: Faber and Faber 1987

Pieterse, J.N. *White On Black: Images of Africa and Blacks in Western Popular Culture* New Haven and London: Yale University Press 1990

Pines, J. *Black and White in Colour*: 'Black people in British Television Since 1936' London BFI 1992

Rees, R. *Fringe First* London: Oberon Books 1992

Rugg, A. *Brickbats and Bouquets* London: Race Today 1984

Sistren *Lionheart Gal* London: Women's Press 1986

Stone, J. *Theatre* West Indian literature Series London: Macmillan 1994

Ugwu, C. (ed.) *Let's Get It On*: 'The Politics of Black Performance' Institute of Contemporary Arts London: Bay Press Seattle 1995

African-American Theatre

Bigsby, C.W.E. *Twentieth Century American Drama Vol 3* 'Beyond Broadway' Cambridge: Cambridge University Press 1985

Bogle, D. *Toms, Coons, Mulattoes, Mammies & Bucks* 'An Interpretive History of Blacks in American Films' New York: Continuum 1992

Case, S.E. *Feminism and Theatre* London: Macmillan 1988

Chinoy, H.L. & Jenkins, L.W. *Women in American Theatre* New York: Theatre communications Group 1981

Dyson, M.E. *Reflecting Black* 'African-American Cultural Criticism' Minneapolis: University of Minnesota 1993

Emery, L. *Black Dance from 1619 to Today* London: Dance Books 1972

Ferguson, R., Gever, M., Minh-ha, T. and West, C. *Out There* 'Marginalisation & Contemporary Cultures' New York: The New Museum of Contemporary Art 1990

Fox, T. *Showtime at the Apollo* London: Quartet 1985

Fusco, C. *English is Broken Here* New York: The New Press 1995

Gilroy, P. *The Black Atlantic* London: Verso 1993

Gray, J. (ed.) *Black Theatre & Performance* 'A Pan-African Bibliography' U.S.A.: Greenwood Press 1990

Hay, S.A. *African-American Theatre:* 'An Historical and Critical Analysis' Cambridge: Cambridge University Press 1994

Hill, E. *The Theatre of Black Americans* (Two Volumes) New Jersey: Prentice Hall 1980. Reprinted by Applause Books (in one volume), London, 1987

Hughes, L. & Meltzer, M. *Black Magic:* 'A Pictorial History of The African-American in the Performing Arts' New York: Da Capo Publications 1990

Jewell, K.S. *From Mammy to Miss America and Beyond* London: Routledge 1993

Johnson, W.J. *Black Manhattan* New York: New Edition Da Capo Press 1991

Kellner, B. (ed.) *The Harlem Renaissance* London: Methuen 1987

Lewis, D.L. *When Harlem was in Vogue* Oxford: Oxford University Press 1981

Long, R.A. *The Black Tradition in American Dance* London: Prion 1989

Mordden. E. *The American Theatre* Oxford: Oxford University Press 1981

Peterson, B.L. *Early Black American Playwrights & Dramatic Writers* 'A Biographical Directory & Catalogue of Plays, Films & Broadcasting Scripts' U.S.A.: Greenwood Press 1990

Sanders, L.S. *The Development of Black Theatre in America* Baton Rouge: Louisiana State University 1988

Williams, M. (ed.) *Black Theatre in the 1960's & 1970's* U.S.A.: Greenwood Press 1985

South African Theatre

Amuta, C. *The Theory of African Literature* London: Zed Books 1989

Banham, M. *African Theatre Today* London: Pitman 1976

Biko, S. *I Write What I like* London: Penguin 1978

Campschrueur, W. & Divendal, J. (ed.) *Culture in another South Africa* London: Zed Books 1989

Coplan, D.B. *In Township Tonight* Harlow: Longman 1986

Davis, G. and Fuchs, A. *Theatre and change in South Africa* Contemporary Theatre Studies: Vol 12, Amsterdam: Harwood Academic Publishers 1996

Fanon, F. *Black Skin, White Masks* London: Pluto 1986

Fuchs, A. *Playing the Market Theatre Johannesburg 1976–1986* Contemporary Theatre Studies: Vol 1, London and Switzerland: Harwood Academic Publishers 1994

Gunner, L. (ed.) *Politics and Performance:* 'Theatre, Poetry and Song in Southern Africa' Johannesburg: Witwatersrand University Press 1994

Kavanagh, R. *Theatre and Cultural Struggle in South Africa* London: Zed Books 1985

Mangariyi, C. *Looking Through the Keyhole* Johannesburg: Raven Press, 1980

Mlama, P.M. *Culture and Development* 'The popular Theatre Approach in Africa' Sweden: Uppsala 1991

Orkin, M. *Drama and the South African State* Manchester: Manchester University Press 1991

Trump, M. (ed.) *Rendering Things Visible* Johannesburg: Ravan Press 1990

West African Theatre

Jeyifo, B. *The Truthful Lie:* 'Essays in a Sociology of African Drama' London: New Beacon Books 1985

Katrak *Wole Soyinka and Modern Tragedy* U.S.A.: Greenwood 1986

Soyinka, W. *Art, Dialogue & Outrage:* 'Essays on Literature and Culture' Nigeria: Ibadan 1988

Performing Arts International
1996, Vol. 1, Part 2, pp. 83–84
Reprints available directly from the publisher
Photocopying permitted by license only

Index

PERFORMING ARTS INTERNATIONAL
AN INTERNATIONAL JOURNAL
Notes for contributors

Submission of a paper will be taken to imply that it represents original work not previously published, that it is not being considered for publication elsewhere and that, if accepted for publication, it will not be published elsewhere in the same form, in any language, without the consent of editor and publisher. It is a condition of acceptance by the editor of a typescript for publication that the publisher automatically acquires the copyright of the typescript throughout the world. It will also be assumed that the author has obtained all necessary permissions to include in the paper items such as quotations, musical examples, figures, tables etc. Permissions should be paid for prior to submission.

Typescripts. Papers should be submitted in triplicate to the Editors, *Performing Arts International* c/o Harwood Academic Publishers, at:

5th Floor, Reading Bridge House	PO Box 27542	3-14-9, Okubo
Reading Bridge Approach	Newark,	Shinjuku-ku
Reading RG1 8PP	or NJ 07101-8742, USA	or Tokyo 169
UK		Japan

Papers should be typed or word processed with double spacing on one side of good quality ISO A4 (212 × 297 mm) paper with a 3 cm left-hand margin. Papers are accepted only in English.

Abstracts and Keywords. Each paper requires an abstract of 100–150 words summarizing the significant coverage and findings, presented on a separate sheet of paper. Abstracts should be followed by up to six key words or phrases which, between them, should indicate the subject matter of the paper. These will be used for indexing and data retrieval purposes.

Figures. All figures (photographs, scheme, charts, diagrams and graphs) should be numbered with consecutive arabic numerals, have descriptive captions and be mentioned in the text. Figures should be kept separate from the text but an approximate position for each should be indicated in the margin of the typescript. It is the author's responsibility to obtain permission for any reproduction from other sources.

Preparation: Line drawings must be of a high enough standard for direct reproduction; photocopies are not acceptable. They should be prepared in black (India) ink on white art paper, card or tracing paper, with all the lettering and symbols included. Computer-generated graphics of a similar high quality are also acceptable, as are good sharp photoprints ("glossies"). Computer print-outs must be completely legible. Photographs intended for halftone reproduction must be good glossy original prints of maximum contrast. Redrawing or retouching of unusable figures will be charged to authors.

Size: Figures should be planned so that they reduce to 12 cm column width. The preferred width of line drawings is 24 cm, with capital lettering 4 mm high, for reduction by one-half. Photographs for halftone reproduction should be approximately twice the desired finished size.

Captions: A list of figure captions, with the relevant figure numbers, should be typed on a separate sheet of paper and included with the typescript.

Musical examples: Musical examples should be designated as "Figure 1" etc., and the recommendations above for preparation and sizing should be followed. Examples must be well prepared and of a high standard for reproduction, as they will not be redrawn or retouched by the printer.

In the case of large scores, musical examples will have to be reduced in size and so some clarity will be lost. This should be borne in mind especially with orchestral scores.

Notes are indicated by superior arabic numerals without parentheses. The text of the notes should be collected at the end of the paper.

References are indicated in the text by date name and the system either "Recent work (Smith & Jones, 1987, Robinson, 1985, 1987) ..." or "Recently Smith & Jones (1987) ..." If a publication has more than three authors, list all names on the first occurence; on subsequent occurrences use the first author's name plus "et al." Use an ampersand rather than "and" between the last two authors. If there is more than one publication by the same author(s) in the same year, distinguish by adding a,b,c etc. to both the text citation and the list of references (e.g. "Smith, 1986a") References should be collected and typed in alphabetical order after the Notes and Acknowledgements sections (if these exist). Examples:

Benedetti, J. (1988) *Stanislavski*, London: Methuen
Granveille-Barker, H. (1934) Shakespeare-s dramatic art. In *A Companion to Shakespeare Studies,* edited by H. Granville-Barker and G. B. Harrison, p. 84. Cambridge: Cambridge University Press
Johnston, D. (1970) Policy in theatre. *Hibernia*, **16**, 16

Proofs. Authors will receive pageproofs (including figures) by air mail for correction and these must be returned as instructed within 48 hours of receipt. Please ensure that a full postal address is given on the first page of the typescript so that proofs are not delayed in the post. Authors' alterations, other than those of a typographical nature, in excess of 10% of the original composition cost, will be charged to authors.

Page Charges. There are no page charges to individuals or institutions.

INSTRUCTIONS FOR AUTHORS

ARTICLE SUBMISSION ON DISK

The Publisher welcomes submissions on disk. The instructions that follow are intended for use by authors whose articles have been accepted for publication and are in final form. Your adherence to these guidelines will facilitate the processing of your disk by the typesetter. These instructions do not replace the journal Notes for Contributors; all information in Notes for Contributors remains in effect.

When typing your article, do not include design or formatting information. Type all text flush left, unjustified and without hyphenation. Do not use indents, tabs or multi-spacing. If an indent is required, please note it by a line space; also mark the position of the indent on the hard copy manuscript. Indicate the beginning of a new paragraph by typing a line space. Leave one space at the end of a sentence, after a comma or other punctuation mark, and before an opening parenthesis. Be sure not to confuse lower case letter "l" with numeral "1", or capital letter "O" with numeral "0". Distinguish opening quotes from close quotes. Do not use automatic page numbering or running heads.

Tables and displayed equations may have to be rekeyed by the typesetter from your hard copy manuscript. Refer to the journal Notes for Contributors for style for Greek characters, variables, vectors, etc.

Articles prepared on most word processors are acceptable. If you have imported equations and/or scientific symbols into your article from another program, please provide details of the program used and the procedures you followed. If you have used macros that you have created, please include them as well.

You may supply illustrations that are available in an electronic format on a separate disk. Please clearly indicate on the disk the file format and/or program used to produce them, and supply a high-quality hard copy of each illustration as well.

Submit your disk when you submit your final hard copy manuscript. The disk file and hard copy must match exactly.

If you are submitting more than one disk, please number each disk. Please mark each disk with the journal title, author name, abbreviated article title and file names.

Be sure to retain a back-up copy of each disk submitted. Pack your disk carefully to avoid damage in shipping, and submit it with your hard copy manuscript and complete Disk Specifications form (see reverse) to the person designated in the journal Notes for Contributors.

Disk Specifications

Journal name _____

_____

Date _____ **Paper Reference Number** _____

Paper title _____

_____

_____

Corresponding author _____

Address _____

_____

_____

_____ **Postcode** _____

Telephone _____

Fax _____

E-mail _____

Disks Enclosed (file names and descriptions of contents)

Text

Disk 1 _____

Disk 2 _____

Disk 3 _____

PLEASE RETAIN A BACK-UP COPY OF ALL DISK FILES SUBMITTED.

GORDON AND BREACH PUBLISHERS   •   HARWOOD ACADEMIC PUBLISHERS

Figures

Disk 1 _____

Disk 2 _____

Disk 3 _____

Computer make and model _____

_____

Size/format of floppy disks

☐ 3.5"   ☐ 5.25"

☐ Single sided   ☐ Double sided

☐ Single density ☐ Double density   ☐ High density

Operating system _____

Version _____

Word processor program _____

Version _____

Imported maths/science program _____

Version _____

Graphics program _____

Version _____

Files have been saved in the following format

Text: _____

Figures: _____

Maths: _____

PLEASE RETAIN A BACK-UP COPY OF ALL DISK FILES SUBMITTED.

GORDON AND BREACH PUBLISHERS   ●   HARWOOD ACADEMIC PUBLISHERS